Mysteries
of the Church

Mysteries of the Church

Miracles of holy mysticism from incorruptible corpses to stigmata

Editor: Peter Brookesmith

Orbis Publishing · London

Acknowledgments
Photographs were supplied by Aldus Archive, Architectural
Association, BBC Hulton Picture Library, Michael Baigent,
Anne Bolsover, Bord Failte, Bridgeman Art Library,
Jonathan Cape, J. Allan Cash, Castelet, Jean-Loup Charmet,
Trustees of Chatsworth Settlement, Frank J. Darmstaedter,
Rene Dazy, Demetrius, Arnold Desser, Colin Edwards,
Mary Evans Picture Library, Werner Forman Archive,
Fortean Picture Library, FOT Library, FOTO EFE,
Editions Gaud, Sonia Halliday, Toby Hogarth, Michael
Holford, Alan Hutchison, L. Macon/Combier, Mancheta/
Pictorial Parade Inc, Mansell Collection, National Council
of Tourism in Lebanon, National Gallery London, Pix
Features, Popperfoto, Prado, Psychic News, Religious News
Service, Rex Features, Roger-Viollet, Royal Library
Copenhagen, St Theresa's Monument, William Sargent,
Betty Saunders, Scala, Barrie M. Schwortz, Smithsonian
Institution/Department of Anthropology, Spectrum Colour
Library, Ed Stuart, Sunday Times Magazine/David Bailey,
Syndication International, Daily Telegraph, Thames and
Hudson, John Topham Library, David Towersey, UPI, Leo
Vala, ZEFA.

Consultants to
The Unexplained
Professor A.J. Ellinson
Dr J. Allen Hynek
Brian Inglis
Colin Wilson
Editorial Director
Brian Innes
Editor
Peter Brookesmith
Deputy Editor
Lynn Picknett
Executive Editor
Lesley Riley
Sub Editors
Mitzi Bales
Chris Cooper
Jenny Dawson
Hildi Hawkins

Picture Researchers
Anne Horton
Paul Snelgrove
Frances Vargo
Editorial Manager
Clare Byatt
Art Editor
Stephen Westcott
Designer
Richard Burgess
Art Buyer
Jean Morley
Production Co-ordinator
Nicky Bowden
Volume Editors
Lorrie Mack
Francis Ritter

© Orbis Publishing Limited, London 1984

First published in the United Kingdom by
Orbis Publishing Limited, London

Marketed in the United States of America by
Jilli Jay Enterprises Inc., Garnerville,
New York 10923, U.S.A.

Material in this publication previously
appeared in the weekly partwork
The Unexplained, © 1980–83

Printed and bound in Yugoslavia by Gorenjski Tisk, Kranj

Contents

Introduction

THE STORY OF CHRIST is nothing less than a history of miracles, from the appearance of the angel before Mary to the resurrection. The man himself was a miracle of insight and wit, pouring out parables, deflecting those who would trap him into political indiscretion, inspiring and upbraiding disciples and disbelievers alike. Miracles also came in his wake: the extraordinary dramatic poetry of the gospels, the miracles of the English language that the translation commissioned by King James has given us, centuries of magnificent painting and sublime music, and the astounding monuments to the glory of God that are the medieval cathedrals of Europe. A message so powerful that it changed history and became a driving force in the affairs of nations for nearly 20 centuries might be expected to wreak effects no less profound in the lives of individuals. The essays in this book look, in the main, at some of the odder phenomena associated with Christianity, while others raise questions about the nature of Jesus of Nazareth himself.

A problem that has vexed scholars in recent decades has been concerned with the possibility that the words of Christ may hide a message or a tradition very different from that now associated with the Church. The discovery of the Dead Sea Scrolls in 1947 produced a rash of theories concerning the background of Christ, ranging from the probability that he was a member of – or certainly very familiar with – the mystical Jewish sect of Essenes, to the somewhat startling assertion that Jesus was really a mushroom – of a psychedelic variety, naturally. The reaction to some of these ideas would have been less surprised had more people been familiar with the *unofficial* Christian texts – the apocryphal gospels. In these, many curious deeds are reported to have been done and many odd utterances said to have been made by Jesus, as if some historical Louella Parsons had been let loose to gather gossip and strange tales about the great man. Whether or not these writings contain any truth – literal, metaphorical or encoded – they were certainly current in the medieval period, episodes from them surviving in folk-song until well into the 20th century, even in rural America.

We can see then, that the picture common people had of Christ and of Christianity was for many centuries a very strange one. And in medieval Europe, it must be remembered, the vast majority of the priesthood was illiterate (as well as slightly pagan) and therefore in no position to judge or control the folklore that was current about Christ.

Exact knowledge of the saints was equally rare. Modern scholarship and research have discovered that many local saints were not historical individuals at all, but refurbished local pagan deities who retained some peculiar characteristics from those previous existences. The medieval mind tended to confuse the issue further by mixing up the saints' curing of sicknesses or afflictions with the ability to inflict them. Thus St Vitus, originally believed to intervene on behalf of those suffering from Sydenham's Chorea, came to be seen as causing it (presumably in retribution for sin).

At this time when perceptions of Christianity were extremely fluid, there was still a vast reservoir of pagan experience and practice among the common people. The greenwood was a mysterious and dangerous place and young ladies entering alone were thought liable to emerge pregnant from the attentions of faeries. Wells, bridges and rivers were all seen as enchanted to some degree. At certain times of the year, especially the equinoxes, the barriers – never very strong – between the Otherworld and this one were considered to be lowered; modern children's Hallowe'en rituals are a faint reminder of this magic-ridden world. The Church occasionally fulminated against all this, though largely in vain: after all, it was itself riddled with paganism – or at least with the same way of thinking that still found paganism so congenial.

In a world perceived in such ambiguous terms, stranded uneasily between different planes of reality and happily blurring the differences between one form of religion and another, miracles and the miraculous were easily accommodated – and equally easily believed. And this was emphatically not a matter of a credulous and simple-minded people eagerly lapping up any fantastic tale that passed their way; such events and accounts fitted exactly into their construction of reality.

Today the Church seems mildly embarrassed about miracles and insists on extremely rigorous evidence before acknowledging their occurrence. Since the Church feels obliged to 'maintain its credibility' in an increasingly sceptical world, this is hardly surprising. What *is* extraordinary is the tenacity of the miraculous tradition among adherents of the Church, who behave in this respect remarkably like citizens of the medieval world. Visions of the Virgin Mary, miraculous healings, the stigmata of Christ – all these and more are visited upon a few, and accepted apparently without a murmur by an enormous number of the devout. Given this continuity, it makes sense that miraculous events, when they occur, should take place within the traditional expectations of the Church.

This raises fundamental questions about miracles. Why do they occur to believers – and why, so often, in the terms that believers would expect? That is to say: do miracles occur in divine response to belief? Or are they in some sense *created* by believers – thus 'explaining' why non-believers so rarely experience them?

The answers to these questions must remain a mystery – by the very nature of the problem. If miracles are (as they so

often *become* to those who experience them) proof given by God of his existence, or of the particular truth of Christianity, then of course they will happen only to believers. If, on the other hand, any given miracle is a product of belief, it could not happen to a non-believer either.

In the pages that follow, most aspects of the miraculous nature of Christianity are discussed. There are the miracles of Christ himself, from the changing of the water into wine at the wedding feast in Cana to the tangled business of the resurrection. In the light of modern psychical research, many of the healings can be seen as relatively 'common' paranormal events. But others are less easy to explain away. Did Jesus walk on the water, or was it an optical illusion, fed by religious zealotry and exaggerated into a paranormal event? Most complex is the matter of the resurrection: central to Christian belief, it can nevertheless be explained in quite everyday terms. Jesus actually hung on the cross for only a few hours – certainly agonising, but not long enough to kill a man. The victim of a crucifixion usually took several *days* to die – of exhaustion, exposure, thirst and, as is related in this volume, of suffocation, rather than from the wounds received. Notwithstanding the effects of the lance that was thrust through his side, the strong possibility that Jesus was alive on being taken down from the cross raises as many questions as it answers. Why did the Romans allow him to be taken down? Was it Pilate's guilty conscience, or was it plain fear of the political consequences? Was someone bribed? If so, why – and why weren't *all* the disciples privy to the secret?

Some of the answers to these questions have been suggested by a remarkable conspiracy theory of Christianity developed by a British research team whose interest in the crucifixion actually started with some strange goings on in the French village of Rennes-le-Château. According to them, Jesus not only survived the crucifixion, but founded a line of descendants that married into the Merovingian dynasty of European kings – and that still survives today. Another interpretation is that the 'myth' of Jesus of Nazareth is a variation on very ancient cosmological and astrological themes, to be understood as metaphor rather than in a fully literal sense.

Whatever actually happened, people have believed in the gospel accounts of the life – and origins – of Christ for a very long time, and what is more they have *acted* on those beliefs. Whether or not they are true, the biblical stories have had exactly the same effect on the devout as if they were meticulously precise records of an historical individual, hence the power to make miracles, raise crusades and build cathedrals.

Side by side with the belief in the historical individual has gone the collecting of relics – indeed a roaring trade has been and is being done in purported splinters of the True Cross, threads from the robe worn at the crucifixion, and various bits of bone and fingernail from a whole gallery of lesser figures in Christian history. Probably the best-known of these today is the Shroud of Turin, which does bear remarkable physical similarities to cloth woven in Palestine when Christ was alive. There is, however, one large objection to the claim that, because of the oddity of the image on the cloth and its likeness to traditional representations of Christ, this was the shroud that wrapped him in the tomb. Anyone who has ever had his fingerprints taken will appreciate this point. An official fingerprint is made by rolling the finger across a pad – and it comes out looking nothing like a fingertip. Cover your face in dye, wrap a cloth around your head, and the cloth will show a similar effect – it won't look much like your face, or anyone else's. However the image on the Turin Shroud got there, it was not simply a result of the cloth being wrapped around a body.

It is when we come to the inexplicable deeds of Christians – and even certain· Christian *artefacts* – that we encounter something closely akin to secular paranormal events. Statues and paintings that bleed and weep apparently real blood and genuine tears are among the most bizarre of this group of phenomena, but these effects may possibly be classified under the heading of psychokinesis – a definition that, even if it is accurate, does not provide an explanation. One may speculate that in each case the effect is somehow caused by the concentrated emotion of many people centred on a particular object; but to go further than that is to enter the realms of faith, rather than science, once again.

Where the rose petals of St Thérèse are concerned, matters are even more complicated. If we could be sure that everyone who benefitted from the saint's post-mortem miracles was aware of Thérèse's history and nature, we might be able to say that the effects were self-induced by sheer faith. But when someone is healed in comparative ignorance of the healing agent – what are we to say then? Despite her ferocious zealotry and somewhat overdeveloped taste for self-mortification (the whip was almost an indulgence to her, it seems), Thérèse did have a down-to-earth side. When it was suggested that, like the corpses of many of the blessed, hers might not decompose, she reportedly exclaimed: 'Oh no! Not *that* miracle!'

Possibly the most intriguing of the effects of belief in Christ is that of the stigmata – wounds in feet, hands and side like those sustained during the crucifixion. Presumably the result of passionate identification with the martyred Jesus, stigmata are startlingly common throughout the history of the Church, occurring at all times and in widely separate places. If they are not a sign directly from God, they are a spectacular example of how the mind can affect matter – or, to put it another way, they present a particularly striking refutation of the notion that mind and matter are entirely separate entities. What needs to be established is whether there are any physical or emotional similarities between stigmatics and more common mortals who develop other kinds of psychosomatic phenomena. But that is only to state in different terms what the Church itself has relatively recently realised: that paranormal events, though they may occur in the worthiest of causes and to unimpeachable witnesses, nonetheless deserve the closest *rational* investigation before they can be claimed for the service of God. Whatever our faith, such study can only further the cause of knowledge and understanding.

PETER BROOKESMITH

Blood and tears

How can a plaster statue of Christ shed real blood, or a painting of the Virgin cry? BOB RICKARD shows that these phenomena have been recorded many times and continue to inspire – and perplex – today

ONE DAY IN APRIL 1975, just after Easter, Mrs Anne Poore of Boothwyn, Pennsylvania, USA, was praying for those who had turned away from the Church. She was kneeling in front of a 26-inch (66-centimetre) plaster statue of Jesus, given to her by a friend the year before. 'Suddenly I looked up at the statue,' she later told reporters, 'and my heart stopped beating. Two ruby-red drops of blood had appeared over the plaster wounds in its palms. I was terrified. I could see it was real blood. Since then, I've seen blood flow from the statue dozens of times.'

It is fashionable today to disbelieve in such things – or rather, to prefer to believe that such things do not happen. The closed or frightened mind characteristically takes refuge behind an exaggerated rationalism. To such entrenched sceptics, accounts of statues, paintings and other objects of religious worship seen weeping tears or issuing blood are evidence of the deplorable survival into this scientific age of primitive and superstitious beliefs. But there is evidence that proves such things do indeed happen, as the following stories show.

In the 1950s, an Italian physician, Dr Piero Casoli, made a prolonged study of weeping Madonnas. There was no shortage, for he concluded that they occurred on average about twice a year in Italy alone. And the records of the British *Fortean Times* show that such occurrences have been recorded throughout history, reports being received from all over the world. For example, in 1527 a statue of Christ in Rome wept copiously and was taken as an omen of the fall of that city. In July 1966 a crucifix owned by Alfred Bolton of Walthamstow, London, shed tears on at least 30 occasions. In December 1960 a statue in a Greek Orthodox church at Tarpon Springs, Florida, streamed 'little teardrops'. And in January 1981 a statue of the Virgin Mary at Caltanissetta, Sicily – said to have wept in 1974 – began to bleed from the right cheek.

Faced with such 'impossible' occurrences, we are prompted to ask the rational question: can these witnesses' stories be dismissed as 'mass hallucinations'? Well-meaning people can sometimes delude themselves – and this is especially true of people in groups sharing a strong emotion such as a religious belief. Yet no one really knows what is meant by the phrase 'mass hallucination'; nor can psychology explain how it works. Nevertheless, there are records of a few cases where people have gathered around a religious image said to bleed or weep, their anticipation fired by rumour, and have 'seen' the miracle, possibly when the most suggestible person present

Above: the 300-year-old wooden crucifix in the church at Porto das Caixas, Brazil, that began to bleed in 1968. The carving became the focus for many miraculous cures, while the 'blood' was tested and proved to be real

Right: the crucifix in the church of St Ignatius in Rome that was seen to ooze drops of blood in 1959

cried out: 'Look, the Madonna is weeping!' The American psychical researcher Raymond Bayless discovered such a case.

It began on the evening of 16 March 1960, when a tinted portrait of the Blessed Virgin Mary began to weep tears inside its glass frame. It was owned by Mrs Pagora Catsounis of New York, who immediately called in her priest, Father George Papadeas, of St Paul's Greek Orthodox Church, Hempstead. He said:

> When I arrived, a tear was drying beneath the left eye. Then, just before our devotions ended, I saw another tear well in her left eye. It started as a small, round globule of moisture in the corner of the eye and slowly trickled down her face.

At the bottom of the frame the slow but steady trickle did not collect, as expected, but appeared to vanish before it had a chance to form a puddle.

In the first week 4000 people filed through Mrs Catsounis's apartment to stare and to pray, while tears flowed intermittently. The painting was then transferred to St Paul's. Then, almost beyond belief, another weeping Madonna turned up in the family. It was owned by an aunt of Mrs Catsounis, Mrs Antonia Koulis. The circumstances seemed suspicious, but the phenomenon was vouched for by the Archbishop himself. The portrait was said to weep copiously, and when Father Papadeas let reporters handle it, it was still damp. Samples of the fluid were taken for analysis and were found not to be human tears. This painting was also enshrined in St Paul's. Mrs Koulis was given a replacement, and this too began to weep.

It was at this point that Raymond Bayless began his investigations, as he reported in the magazine *Fate* in March 1966. Close examination of the surface of the painting revealed stains below the eyes that consisted of crystallised particles something like those of a serum. The accumulations, being dried, had not moved downwards. When Bayless

Above: the plaster statue that began to bleed from the hands in April 1975 in the home of Mrs Anne Poore of Boothwyn, Pennsylvania, USA. Since then it has bled every Friday and has become the centre piece of a shrine where it draws large crowds

Below left: Archbishop Takovos, head of the Greek Orthodox Church of America, inspects an icon of the Virgin Mary that was reported to have shed tears in the home of the Catsounis family in New York in 1960

Below right: another weeping Madonna in the Catsounis family was discovered within weeks of the first. This was found to shed an 'oily' substance

examined the image a second time these raised 'tears' were still in the same place. He found no pinholes or other openings through which liquid could have been introduced into the central area of the painting. He stated:

> During our first visit . . . one woman, who was acting as interpreter, suddenly cried out that a new tear was descending from an eye. I looked immediately but in my opinion such was absolutely not the case. . . . Some viewers and worshippers were convinced they saw tears appear and move on the surface of the icon while my friend and I were both present. On the other hand, we both were convinced, because of our careful examination, that . . . the tear was not liquid and did not flow or even descend a fraction of an inch.

The case of Mrs Poore's bleeding statue is quite different. When she recovered from her shock at its sudden bleeding, she made the statue the centre piece of a shrine on her front porch where a great many people saw it. On Fridays and holy days the flow of blood was

particularly strong, streaming downwards, in a cyclical recurrence that parallels the regular bleedings of some well-documented stigmatics. Eventually the statue was moved to St Luke's Episcopalian Church at Eddystone, Pennsylvania, and installed on a platform 10 feet (3 metres) above the altar. Father Chester Olszewski, pastor of the church, said: 'It has bled as long as four hours. I know there can be no trickery. I have seen the palms dry, then, minutes later have observed droplets of blood welling out of the wounds. . . . Incredibly the blood seldom runs off the statue. Its robes are now encrusted with dried blood.' Another priest, Father Henry Lovett, said he came to see it as a sceptic and went away convinced it was a miracle. 'I've personally taken the hands off the statue – they are held in place by wooden dowels – and examined them. They're solid chalk. And the statue has bled profusely even as I watched.'

Blood of great age?

In this case there is no doubt that a blood-like liquid flowed mysteriously from the sites of Christ's wounds on the statue. But was it actually blood? Dr Joseph Rovito, a respected Philadelphia physician, conducted his own investigation. x-rays could find no trace of a reservoir or other trick mechanism concealed in the statue, but the result of the blood tests was not so straightforward. Although identified as human blood, the low red cell count was curious, and indicated great age. The fact that the blood flowed quite a distance before coagulating indicated that it was fairly fresh, and fresh blood contains millions of red cells. Dr Rovito concluded: 'It's so old we can't even determine the blood type.' Father Lovett, and other Catholics, jumped to the conclusion that this was actually the blood of Christ.

Such images are almost always objects of worship, and so the mysterious appearance of liquids on or near these images is bound to be interpreted in a religious context. But outside the context there are almost identical accounts of a variety of related phenomena: bleeding tombstones; persistently wet or recurring bloodstains in a few haunted houses (evidence of a legendary murder, perhaps); or the constant distillation of clear oils or blood-like fluids from the incorrupt relics of some saints (see page 31).

Once trickery and natural explanations such as condensation have been discounted, and the flow of blood has been established as not coming from inside the statue, then we have to accept that the liquid is appearing on the surface of the object, materialised there from an unknown source by a mysterious force called – for want of a better term – teleportation. The same probably applies to the appearance of tears on statues or icons. Yet the appearances of these liquids are not random; in fact, they are remarkably consistent, for they restrict themselves to the

In September 1911 a portrait of Christ in the church at Mirebeau-en-Poitou in France began to ooze blood (A). By Christmas of that year blood was flowing from both palms, head and from the stylised heart (B). In March 1912 the blood was flowing copiously (C). The phenomenon seemed in some way connected with the parish priest, Abbé Vachère. Consecrated hosts bled as he blessed them, and a nearby statue of the Virgin Mary wept. Much to his superiors' displeasure he revelled in the attention of the pilgrims who flocked to witness the phenomena and he was eventually excommunicated. The portrait stopped bleeding (D) at his death in 1915

appropriate sites where either faith or legend leads us to expect miraculous happenings. Further regularity is observed in the association between bleeding and images of Christ, and weeping and images of the Virgin Mary. This regular association suggests either that the teleportative force is created by an unknown intelligence or that it acts automatically in response to especially powerful images in the human mind, on an instinctive or unconscious level. It seems probable that the undoubted piety of Mrs Poore, in her Easter devotions, should have brought forth such 'real' evidence of the sufferings of Christ.

Another American parapsychologist, the writer D. Scott Rogo, tells the story of the Reverend Robert Lewis, who, on the day of his ordination, recalled how his grandmother – his first spiritual mentor – had wept with joy the day he said he wanted to join the ministry. She had died before his ordination and he deeply regretted not being able to share the happiness of his success with her. He glanced at her photograph on his dresser, and suddenly accused his companion of playing a joke. The friend, the Reverend William Raucher, later wrote:

> I went over to see what was troubling him. I was astounded. The photo of Bob's grandmother was soaking wet, dripping with a small pool of water spreading on the dresser under it. Examining the picture we found that it was wet *inside* the glass. . . . The back of the picture, made of dyed imitation velvet, was so wet the velvet had streaked and faded. Removed from its frame, the photo didn't dry quickly. When it did dry, the area about the face remained puffed, as though the water had originated there and run downwards from the eyes.

Grandmother cries again

Rogo suggests that Lewis had unconsciously used a telekinetic ability to project a strong emotion into his immediate environment. 'Lewis underwent a mini-trauma when he passed his ordination exams,' writes Rogo. 'His grandmother often wept with joy . . . He wanted to share his joy with [her]; he wanted to see her cry with happiness, so he used his psychic ability to stage the event.' He makes the further suggestion that this was not a freakish power of one individual, but that we all may possess this ability to cause dogmatic changes in our environment by projecting powerfully felt or suppressed emotions.

This type of paranormal projection, in which the events seem significantly related to the spiritual or psychological tensions of those involved, takes two classic forms: overtly religious phenomena, and the disturbances known as poltergeist activity. In both cases, contemporary theorists relate the outburst of activity, or sudden manifestation of phenomena, to some inner crisis. This crisis may take many forms, such as the onset of puberty and its attendant physical and emotional complications, or the mounting pressures of illness, frustrations and inadequacies that finally reach an explosive release by being projected as 'poltergeists'. Or the final explosion of psychic frustrations can take the form of religious conversion, ecstasies, or visions.

An example of the latter happened in May 1979 in New Mexico, where an ordinary plastic-coated postcard-sized portrait of Jesus wept tears of genuine blood. The religious memento had been bought in 1972 by Mrs Kathy Malott for her grandmother, Mrs Willie Mae Seymore. On 25 May Mrs Malott and her husband Zach were visiting Mrs Seymore when Mr Malott noticed a small dark drop forming on the picture, just under the right eye. It quickly turned into a steady stream, forming a puddle at the bottom, where it was tucked into the frame of a larger painting. 'The blood was running from the picture just as if I had cut my

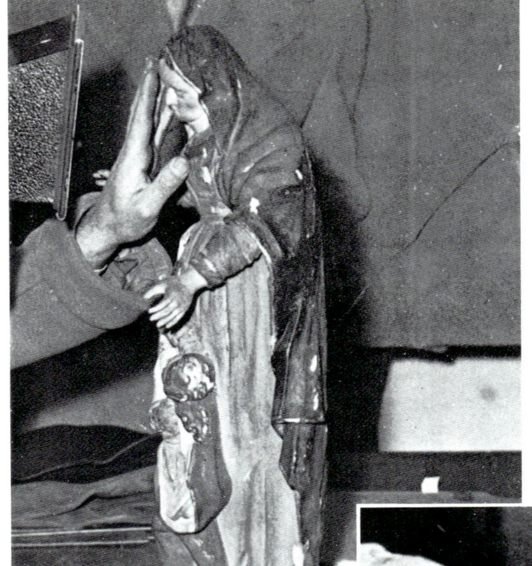

Left: a statue of St Anne belonging to Jean Salate, a hotel owner of Entrevaux in France. Its finger had begun to ooze blood (below) after Salate had broken it in a fit of anger in 1954. The finger bled 30 drops during the day and again the next morning. Crowds of the pious and the curious gathered to venerate the statue. Although chemical analysis proved that the blood was real, rumour spread that Salate had faked it

Below: the bronze statue of an aristocratic Japanese lady owned by Allen Demetrius of Pittsburgh, USA, that began to cry just 10 days before the nuclear accident at Three Mile Island, Pennsylvania in 1979. She had been known to weep only once before – on 6 August 1945, the night that an atomic bomb was dropped on Hiroshima. Demetrius said: 'It was like she was crying about the bombing.' Thousands of people travelled to witness the oxidised stains on the face of 'the weeping bronze of Hiroshima'

finger,' said Mrs Seymore. Mrs Malott went to wipe it off but, somewhat awed by the occurrence, other members of the family prevented her and decided to call a priest. One declined to come. As the news spread and reporters came to the house, many examined the postcard portrait and could find no cut or hole through which a liquid could appear. The blood seemed to flow directly from the surface of the plastic. Later the substance was given a standard blood test – a 'hematest' – at the Eastern New Mexico Medical Center Hospital in Roswell. A spokesman said: 'Yes, it was honest-to-gosh, bonafide blood.' An even more bizarre note was added when the blood was discovered to be still uncongealed after 24 hours.

Perhaps the most intriguing fact was that the flow had only just begun when Zach Malott noticed it. It is almost as though the phenomenon was waiting for attention before it began in earnest.

There is also an interesting sequel: four nights later Zach Malott had a vivid dream in which Christ appeared and told him that the blood was a sign of his Second Coming. Prior to this Mr Malott had told reporters his family were 'not too religious'. Now, he said, his whole outlook had changed. 'I was a sinner. Now I'm going to follow Jesus Christ.' Had the mysterious bleeding sparked the change in him or, conversely, had it been a sign of his inner conversion?

A more demonstrable case of bizarre cause

and effect involves the celebrated weeping Madonna of Syracuse, Sicily, in August 1953. The statue was owned by the newly wed Mrs Antonietta Janusso and was in fact a small plaster bust of the Virgin Mary in the style known as 'The Immaculate Heart of Mary', and was a wedding gift, a mass-produced ornament bought locally.

The couple were desperately poor, and sharing accommodation in an extremely run-down quarter of the city. Mrs Janusso began to suffer mysterious illnesses. Some months into pregnancy she experienced fits and convulsions, with alternating periods of blindness, deafness and dumbness. Doctors thought it was some kind of toxemia but could find no cause. (However, similarity between her symptoms and those of clinical hysteria have been noted by some researchers.)

The bedridden girl, in a sorry state, looked up one day to the shelf above the bed where the statue rested, and saw it begin to cry. It continued to do so for many days and was seen by impeccable witnesses. But at the end of the first day, despite the excitement and strain of people crowding into the small room to see for themselves, Mrs Janusso felt considerably better. By the time the statue had stopped crying, she had completely recovered.

To the faithful it was a miracle – to others it was confirmation that her illnesses, genuinely debilitating though they were, had a hysterical origin. Perhaps the unconscious stages such apparently mystical or magical events to break a vicious circle of depression and self-pity. As Dr Fodor said about the Catsounis case: 'The tears stopped when the reasons for self-pity were removed by blessing and return to health.'

Many of the people unfortunate enough to be the focus of poltergeist phenomena also suffer from similar traumas, crises or changes. Mary Jobson, a 13-year-old poltergeist victim investigated in 1839 by Dr Reid Clanny, suffered patches of anaesthesia on her skin, swellings, and convulsions, while

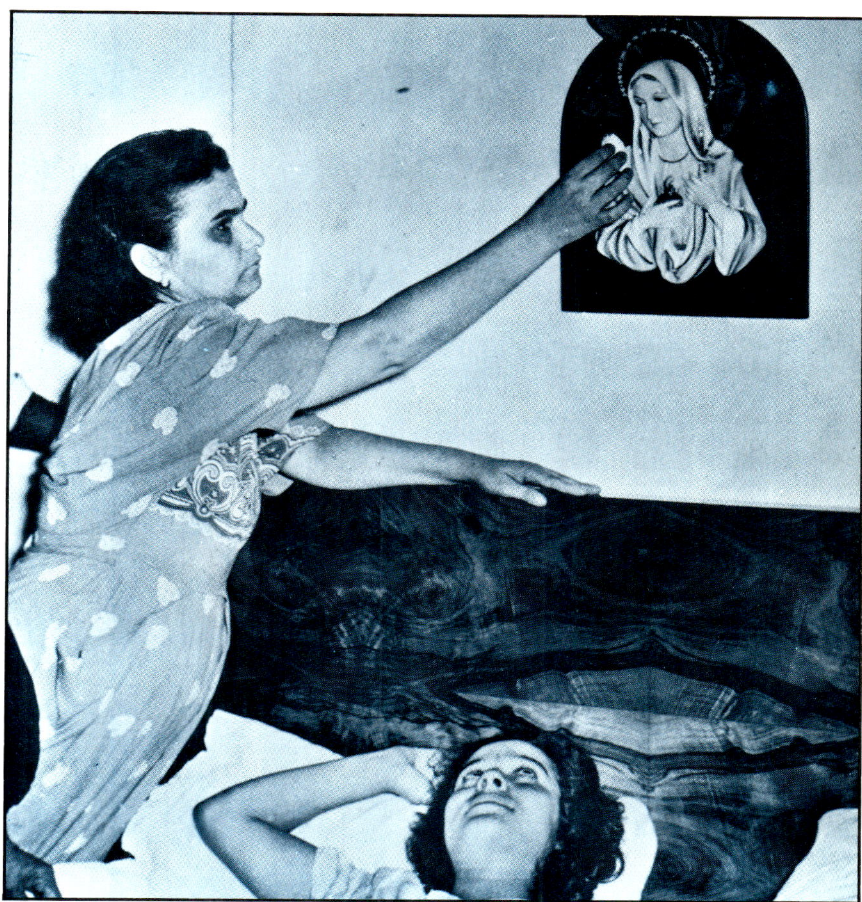

Above: Mrs Antonietta Janusso lies on her sickbed in Syracuse, Sicily, in 1953 while her mother wipes away the tears shed by the plaster Madonna. She recovered completely after the statue stopped crying

Below left: the Madonna of the Sicilian village of Caltanissetta that was seen to shed tears in 1974 and bled from a cheek in 1980. These 'flows' persisted under rigorous scrutiny

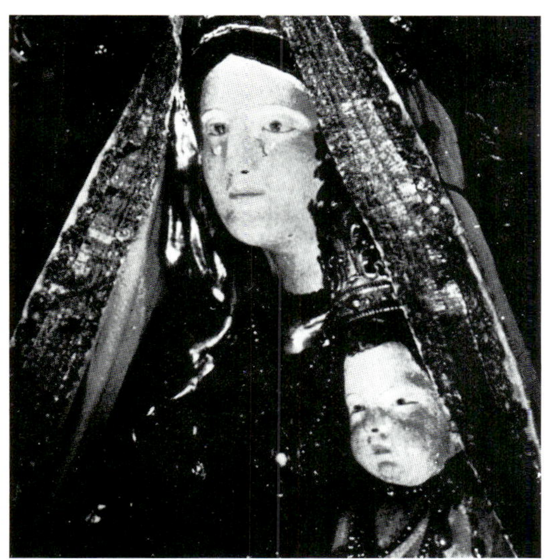

her bedroom furniture moved, music and voices came from mid-air as well as raps from the walls. At times quantities of water fell 'from nowhere' onto the floor.

Many more cases could be cited, but one particularly worthy of mention, which occurred in Ireland in 1920, seems to display overlapping characteristics of both the religious and the poltergeist type of projection. It centred on a devout 16-year-old boy, James Walsh, of Templemore, Tipperary, in whose home all the holy pictures and statuary began to ooze blood. A hollow in the earthen floor of his room kept filling with water, no matter how many times it was emptied. It was said that thousands of people took away containers of the water. The family was also tormented by mobile furniture and other forms of psychokinesis.

Of all the rich and intriguing range of paranormal phenomena Fodor thought the subject of bleeding and weeping images deserved 'a class of its own'. It happens – but we can only guess at how or why. The facts are suggestive of a teleportation of liquids – but from where? And in the end the value of these phenomena must, like those associated with poltergeists, be studied in their relationship to the person who proves to be their focus. But the results are very different, for as Fodor observed: 'Religious ecstasy of the Weeping Madonna type restores, whereas the poltergeist senselessly frightens and destroys.'

In the course of two or three years, Bérenger Saunière went from being a penniless village curé to one of the richest men of the region. Within his church door he raised a lifesize figure of a devil. BRIAN INNES explores the mysteries of Rennes-le-Château

FROM THE SOUTHERN French city of Carcassonne to the Spanish border, the hills rise steadily to the peaks of the Pyrenees. The area is now sparsely populated, with small towns and tiny villages, a land of minor vineyards between the bare stone ridges, of deserted valleys loud with nightingales, of rushing streams fed from the melting snows, and wild sandy uplands rich with thyme and myrtle. But once it was extensively settled – by the southern Gauls, a Celtic people whose capital of Narbo is now Narbonne, and later by the Visigoths, whose kingdom of Septimania survived from AD 475 until it was overrun by the Moors in 715. Ruined watchtowers and tumbledown castles dominate the hilltops, evidence of the troubled condition of the region through 10 centuries.

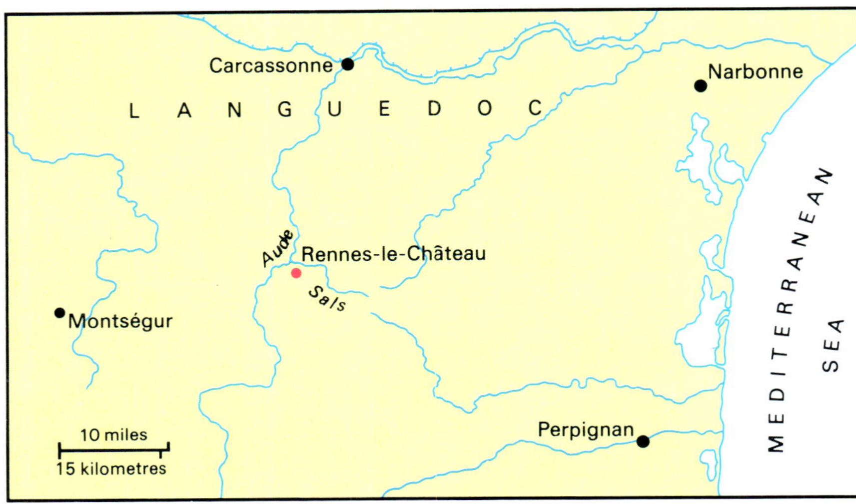

This is the southern half of the Languedoc, which from the 1050s came under the rule of the counts of Toulouse, autonomous vassals of the king of France. It was also the heartland of the Catharist heresy – often known as the Albigensian heresy from its prevalence among the inhabitants of the city of Albi – and on the steep bare rock of Montségur the Cathars made their last desperate stand in 1244.

The ancient town of Aereda, known to the Romans as Rhedae, a few miles to the east of Montségur, gave its name to the region of Rhedesium, now called Razès. Once it was a capital with more than 30,000 inhabitants, its hilltop castle guarding the confluence of the rivers Aude and Sals. Today it is a decayed hamlet, its few houses clinging to the single steep street and overlooking a wild, deserted plateau. This is Rennes-le-Château.

Top: the Tour Magdala, built by Bérenger Saunière on the western edge of the ramparts of Rennes-le-Château

Above: the southern corner of France below the Pyrenees and the border with Spain is known as Languedoc-Roussillon. Here, among the rocky uplands of the Corbières, was the heartland of the Cathar heretics

In 1885, at the age of 33, François-Bérenger Saunière was appointed curé of the tiny church of Sainte-Madeleine, which stood, neglected and in poor repair, at the top of the village street, where once the Visigoths had raised a mighty fortified palace. A man of humble origins, the eldest of seven children, Saunière had no future except in the Church. Like many of his fellow priests, he took into his house a young girl, Marie Denarnaud, as a housekeeper and settled down to a prospect of lifelong penny-pinching obscurity. But fate decreed otherwise.

Saunière learned that one of his predecessors had left a small legacy for the upkeep of the church, and in 1892 he decided to restore the church altar. This was made from a solid stone slab, one end of which was cemented into the wall of the church, while the other was supported on an ancient carved stone column that had survived from the times of the Visigoths. When the slab was lifted, the column was found to be hollow; inside were three wooden tubes, sealed with wax, which held four parchment manuscripts.

Copies of these parchments have survived. At first glance they seem to be nothing more than transcriptions of well-known New Testament passages, written in Latin in a strange archaic-looking script. The first (John 12:1–12) describes Christ's visit to Bethany – the house of Lazarus, Martha and Mary Magdalene. The second is the story of the disciples plucking ears of corn on the sabbath; but it has been put together from three different versions, those of Matthew (12:1-8), Mark (2:23-28) and Luke (6:1-5).

On closer inspection, however, these manuscripts reveal a number of unexpected features: there are distinctive monogrammatic devices, additional letters have been added to the text, some letters are marked with a dot, others are displaced – in fact, there are all the signs that these manuscripts are ciphered. And indeed, in the hands of cryptographers, they yield to decipherment.

At the beginning of 1893 Saunière took the manuscripts to his bishop, Monseigneur Félix-Arsène Billard, in Carcassonne, and was given permission (and money) to go at once to Paris. There he laid the documents before Abbé Bieil, the director of Saint-Sulpice, who introduced him to his nephew, the religious publisher Ané, at whose home Saunière lodged while he was in Paris, and to his grand-nephew Émile Hoffet, destined to become a famous authority on old manuscripts and secret societies.

For just three weeks Saunière remained in Paris. He spent much of his time in the Louvre, where he bought reproductions of three apparently unrelated paintings: Poussin's *The shepherds of Arcadia*, David Teniers's portrayal of Saint Anthony, and a portrait of Pope St Celestine V by an unknown hand. He also became the friend – remarkable for a humble parish priest from a

Above: the slab, with its archaic carved scene, that Saunière removed from the church altar. There are many unconfirmed stories concerning what he found buried below the slab – rumours mentioned two skeletons, and a pot full of 'worthless medallions'

remote corner of France – of the toast of Paris, Emma Calvé. This beautiful operatic soprano was then at the height of her career: renowned for her interpretations of Carmen and of Marguerite in Gounod's *Faust*, she had just returned from an outstanding season in London, during which she had been invited to Windsor by Queen Victoria. For many years she remained a close friend of Saunière, and visited him regularly until her

At the centre of the web

The Catharist heresy was what is known as a 'dualist' belief – often called Manichaean during the Middle Ages, after the teachings of a Persian named Mani. Dualism is an attempt to explain the existence of evil: the material world is believed to be the creation of the Demiurge, an evil spirit who has created Man in his own image, while God, who has given Man the knowledge of good and the opportunity to save himself, is not omnipotent. So, to be saved, Man must remove himself from all material things: he must give up his bodily needs, including marriage and procreation, deny all temporal power, and, in the end, face the knowledge that there is no other course open for him than his own death.

In the eighth century the dualist heresy reached Europe, and in the 10th a humble Bulgarian priest named Bogomil established an influential church. Its members avoided procreation by practising homosexuality, and the fact that they came from Bulgaria led soon to their being known as 'buggers'. By way of northern Italy dualism penetrated most of western Europe in the 12th century: its followers were divided into believers and initiates and some of the initiates took the word Cathar, from the Greek for 'purified', to describe themselves. The creed attracted many adherents because it stressed the Christian

values of humility and charity at a time when Churchmen were infamous for their venality.

The Church soon recognised the danger in the dualist heresy, and took strong measures to stamp it out. But in the Languedoc, where it enjoyed some measure of protection from the counts of Toulouse, Catharism persisted into the 13th century. In 1208 Pope Innocent III proclaimed a crusade against the Albigensians, and an army of some 40,000 – which included Simon de Montfort the Elder – set out from Lyon in July 1209. For 20 years the campaigns flowed back and forth across the Languedoc, until in 1229 the French throne secured the final humiliation of the Count of Toulouse and took over his lands.

Now the heresy had to be rooted out by the officers of the Inquisition. Gradually they drove the Cathars further into the wilderness until their only refuge was the fortress of Montségur, on an almost sheer rock rising some 500 feet from the surrounding plain. In 1243, several thousand royal troops laid siege to the fortress, and on 2 March 1244 the Cathars finally surrendered. Two months earlier, steps had been taken to guard the Cathar treasures – 'gold, silver, and a great quantity of money' – and on the night before the surrender three or four heretics were secretly lowered down the rock face to organise its disposal. Nothing more was heard of them or of the treasure. . . .

An order of heretics

Saint-Sulpice is the largest church in Paris after Notre-Dame, and in the 19th century its Seminary was one of the principal training establishments for the French priesthood. Among its more notorious alumni at this period was Alphonse Louis Constant, who abandoned the priesthood and later took the name of Eliphas Lévi. Under this name he published *Dogma and ritual of high magic*, and a number of other books of avowedly Rosicrucian doctrine.

Another apostate clergyman was Abbé Joseph-Antoine Boullan, who in 1876 announced himself as High Priest of the Church of Carmel, in Lyon. Two young Parisians, the Marquis Stanislas de Guaita and his companion Oswald

Wirth who were disciples of Lévi, joined the Church of Carmel in order to learn its secret rituals and then, in 1887, announced that Boullan was a 'condemned man'.

Convinced that Guaita and Wirth intended to kill him by occult means, Boullan enlisted the support of the novelist J.-K. Huysmans, who drew a sympathetic portrait of the ex-Abbé in his novel about black magic, *Là-Bas*. One of Huysmans' friends, a former disciple of Boullan, was the writer Jules Bois, who at that time was the lover of singer Emma Calvé. When, on 4 January 1893, after writing a letter full of forebodings of death, Boullan suddenly dropped dead, Bois immediately published a letter in a Paris newspaper accusing Guaita of having murdered him by magic. A few days later, Saunière arrived in Paris. . . .

marriage in 1914 to the tenor Gasbarri.

On his return to Rennes, Saunière continued his restoration work on the church. With the assistance of some young men from the village – one of whom was still alive in 1962 and provided invaluable details of the curé's activities – he raised another stone slab, which lay directly in front of the altar. The underside of the slab was found to be carved in an archaic style identified as dating from the sixth or seventh century.

There are two scenes on the slab, which take place either in an arched building or in a crypt. That on the left represents, as far as it is possible to tell, a mounted knight sounding a hunting horn while his horse lowers its head to drink at a fountain. That on the right is of another knight with a staff in one hand and in the other either a child upon his saddle-bow or a disc or sphere of some sort. The stone is worn and chipped in places, and it is difficult to identify the subjects clearly, but there is no doubt as to the great age of the work.

After the slab had been removed, Saunière ordered the youths to dig down for several feet, but when they announced that they had discovered something in their excavations he sent them home and locked himself in the church. It is said that they had uncovered two skeletons and a pot full of bright objects, which Saunière told them were worthless medallions; and certainly, when a further excavation was made much later, a skull was found with a characteristic ritual slot made in the cranium.

After this discovery, work ceased in the church for some time. Instead, Saunière, accompanied by his housekeeper Marie, took to wandering the surrounding countryside, a sack on his back. Each evening he returned, the sack loaded with stones that he had selected with care, and when he was asked the purpose of his excursions, he replied that

Above: two improbable lovers – the humble Abbé Saunière and world-famous singer Emma Calvé

Right: on the Visigothic pillar that he took from the church, Saunière raised a cheap statue from Lourdes. On the canopy over it are the words 'Penitence, penitence'

he had decided to beautify the tiny garden in front of the church with a stone grotto. Certainly the grotto is still there, although sadly reduced; it has been ransacked, either by souvenir hunters or by those who hoped that the stones might reveal Saunière's secret.

But this was not his only strange pastime. The cemetery of the church contained two memorial stones marking the grave of Marie de Negri d'Ables (died 1781), the wife of Francis d'Hautpoul, the *seigneur* of Rennes. By night, Saunière moved these stones from one end of the cemetery to the other, and patiently erased the inscriptions. Unknown to him, however, his labours were in vain, for

the inscriptions had already been copied by itinerant archaeologists – and one of the stones, we now know, bore the same monogrammatic device as appeared in at least one of the manuscripts.

For the next two years, Bérenger Saunière spent much of his time travelling. He is known to have opened two bank accounts in neighbouring cities, one in Perpignan and one in Toulouse, another in Paris, and a fourth has been traced as far away as Budapest. From Germany, Spain, Switzerland and Italy, money orders arrived frequently for Marie Denarnaud, some apparently sent by various religious communities.

Then, from 1896, Saunière undertook a major refurbishment of the church, the results of which can be seen to this day. The overall effect is extraordinary. Fitting diagonally into the junction of nave and transept he laid a checker-board floor of 64 alternate black and white square tiles; beside the entrance door he raised a huge garishly coloured monument, the stoup borne upon the head of a wildly staring lifesize figure of the demon Asmodeus, while above rise small statues of four winged angels, with the motto *Par ce signe tu le vaincras* – 'In this sign shalt thou conquer' – a quotation from the vision that brought about Emperor Constantine's conversion to Christianity in AD 313.

'This is a fearful place'

The walls of the church are covered with painted relief scenes in popular style – a rather unconventional series of the Stations of the Cross, and, above the confessional, a representation of Christ on the Mount. Saunière himself painted the picture of Mary Magdalene for the front of the altar. Strangest of all, carved above the porch of the church are the words of Jacob at Bethel, spoken the morning after he had seen the vision of angels ascending and descending a ladder that led to Heaven: *Terribilis est locus iste*, 'This is a fearful place'.

When work in the church was finished, Saunière did not give up his lust to rebuild. He purchased the land that extended between the church and the western edge of the hill. Along the crest he built a semicircular promenade, and at its southern end a two-storied tower, the Tour Magdala. Within the curve of the raised walk he created a formal garden, and at the eastern end, separated by a small courtyard from the church, he built a guesthouse that he named Bethania.

Saunière paid for all this work from his own pocket. And when Bethania was finished, and furnished with valuable antiques, he entertained his guests royally, with fine wines and rich food. There were regular visits from Emma Calvé, whenever her professional engagements would allow; and other guests included the secretary of state for fine arts, the writer Andrée Bruguière, many local notables – and, now and again, strictly incognito, a man whispered to be the

Habsburg archduke John, a cousin of the Austrian Emperor.

When Saunière died in 1917, it is calculated that he had spent well over one million francs – and these were *francs d'or*, worth about 20 times a present-day franc. After his death, and for 36 years until her own death in 1953, Marie Denarnaud wanted for nothing, and in a letter in 1920 she estimated her own fortune at more than 100,000 francs. Between 1885 and 1893, then, Bérenger Saunière was transformed from the poor curé of an impoverished parish into an enormously wealthy man – one of the most extravagant spendthrifts of the region. The evidence of his expenditure is there, in Rennes-le-Château, for all to see, even if it has faded somewhat with the years. But where did Saunière's riches come from?

Below: the porch of the Church of Sainte-Madeleine at Rennes-le-Château. Among a number of biblical quotations, the decorative keystone above the arch is engraved *Terribilis est locus iste*, 'This is a fearful place'. Notice also the signs stencilled on the tympan, which have been identified as alternating crosses and roses

In search of ancient gold

For centuries, legends have told of a fabulous treasure buried somewhere in the Razès region of southern France. Did Bérenger Saunière discover it in the 1890s, and what exactly was the treasure?

THE STORIES OF the golden treasure of Rennes-le-Château are many and persistent, and some, at least, are true. To begin with, the area is rich in minerals, and lead and silver, copper and gold have been mined there since Roman times. In the 12th century the Grand Master of the Knights Templar was Bertrand de Blanchefort, whose castle stood on a rocky spur within sight of Rennes; and he brought labourers all the way from Germany to dig gold from his mines.

But local tradition tells a different story. If we can believe César d'Arcons, an engineer who, five centuries later, was sent to report on mining in the Razès region, these Germans were not miners but goldsmiths; and the local historian Louis Fédié wrote, in 1880:

> The people of the Middle Ages believed that the precious metals extracted from the Blanchefort mine came, not from a vein in the rock, but from a store of gold and silver ingots buried in the dungeons of the fortress by its first masters, the Visigothic kings.

Then there are the tales of remarkable discoveries, like that made by the young shepherd Ignace Paris in 1645. Seeking a lost lamb, he tumbled into a hidden ravine that

The triumphal arch of Titus Flavius in Rome clearly shows the great *menorah*, the silver trumpets and what may be the Ark of the Covenant, all from Solomon's Temple

led into a cave lined with skeletons and piled with gold. But when he returned to Rennes with a hat full of this gold, the villagers accused him of theft, refused to believe his tale, and stoned him to death.

More recently, close by Rennes, a slab of gold weighing nearly 45 pounds (20 kilograms) was found, made from fused Arab (or, more likely Crusader state) coins; and an ingot of 110 pounds (50 kilograms) was found shortly after. In 1928, the remains of a large gold statue were found in the ruins of a hut on the edge of the stream that flows below

And the Lord said unto Moses...

'Thou shalt make a candlestick of pure gold; of beaten work shall the candlestick be made; his shaft, and his branches, his knops and his flowers, shall be of the same. And six branches shall come out of the sides of it; three branches of the candlestick out of the one side, and three branches of the candlestick out of the other side. . . . And in the candlestick shall be four bowls made like unto almonds . . . all it shall be one beaten work of pure gold. And thou shalt make the seven lamps thereof; and they shall light the lamps thereof, that they may give light over against it. . . . Of a talent of pure gold shall he make it, with all these vessels, and look that thou make them after their pattern, which was shewed thee in the mount. . . .'

(A talent is approximately 110lbs/50kg)

Rennes; it had been partly melted away, but its feet were still clearly distinguishable.

Where would this gold have come from? Over the past 2000 years, four major cultures have flourished in the region, and all four have shared a preoccupation with gold as a precious metal. To the Celts it was a metal of magic properties: unlike iron or copper, it came from the earth shining and immutable, hard to work but unchanged by the atmosphere or the conditions of the forge, and was the living symbol of regal power and priestly mystery.

For the Romans, on the other hand, gold was the prize of empire. They subdued the Celts, and all the other peoples of the frontier regions from Spain in the west to Persia in the east; they seized their golden ornaments and took over their mines, and they carried all their booty back to Rome.

The Visigoths, less sophisticated than the Romans, looked on gold much as the Celts had done. Their kings, queens and princes wore gold to symbolise both their power and their wealth; and, Christian converts as they were, they also used the gold to make and decorate their sacred objects.

Then came the people of the Languedoc. For them gold was, above all else, an article of commerce. Many of the crusading knights came from the south of France, and they

Above: a Visigothic cross, of a type now known as a 'Templar cross', from Rennes-le-Château church

Left: a Templar seal. Compare the two men on one horse with the figures on the slab taken from the church floor (page 15)

Below: the al-Aqsa mosque, and the crypt of Solomon's Temple in Jerusalem

had summoned the hosts of Israel, the Ark of the Covenant, the golden table of the Shewbread, and the great seven-branched candlestick or *menorah*, made from some 110 pounds (50 kilograms) of solid gold.

The triumphal arch of Titus in Rome clearly shows this heavy object being borne away from the temple on the shoulders of Titus's men, and it was lodged in the Temple of Peace in the Forum of Vespasian. What later happened to it is the subject of a number of conflicting stories. The first tells how, when Maxentius was fleeing from Constantine in 312, it fell from the Milvian bridge into the Tiber and (rather unbelievably) was lost. A second reports that, when Alaric the Visigoth sacked Rome in 410, he carried it off as part of his booty.

The third story, to which we shall return later, maintains that the Jerusalem treasure was taken in 455 by Gaiseric the Vandal from Rome to North Africa. In the following century the Byzantine general Belisarius recovered it and carried it to Constantinople, and the emperor Justinian restored it to Jerusalem, where it was placed in a Christian shrine. But in 615 the Persians sacked Jerusalem, and since that time nothing more has been heard of the treasure.

Alaric died in the same year as his sack of Rome, and he was succeeded by Ataulphūs,

brought back booty from the East.

For the moment, we may discount the Celts and the Romans. Very little Celtic gold has ever been discovered, and no doubt the Romans took all they could find, as they took most precious objects, back to Rome. But the Visigoths present us with a fascinating mystery.

Among the greatest treasures that the Romans had carried back to Rome were the sacred objects of Solomon's Temple in Jerusalem. In AD 69 Titus Flavius, the elder son of the emperor Vespasian, led a campaign against the Jews, who had revolted against Roman rule. In September 70 he took Jerusalem and sacked the temple, taking the silver trumpets with which the sons of Aaron

who led the Visigoths to settle in southern Gaul and Spain. It is well known that at this time they possessed a great deal of treasure, which was made up of two distinct parts. One comprised the personal jewels of the kings and the accumulated tributes that they had levied; this was used to cover public expenditure, and was lodged at Toulouse. The other, known as the Old Treasure, was made up of the booty won by the Visigoths during their wanderings. It was eventually lodged at Carcassonne during the seventh century, and included the great gold Missorium of some 45 pounds (20 kilograms), the Emerald tablet with its three rows of pearls and 60 golden feet, and, most probably, the *menorah* of Jerusalem.

When Clovis, the king of the Franks, threatened Carcassonne in 507, the Old Treasure was removed to Ravenna, but it was returned to the Visigothic king Amalaric when he came of age. Part of this treasure, a small part, was taken by the Franks when they captured Narbonne in the seventh century, but a major part was carried by the Visigoths to their Spanish capital of Toledo. When the Moors took the city in 711, it is known that they captured the famous Missorium, but much of the treasure was lost until the 19th century, when it was discovered in a hoard at Guarrazar, not far from Toledo. It included nine magnificent votive crowns of gold ornamented with sapphires, but not the *menorah*. 'Shall we one day discover in France,' wrote H-P Eydoux in his *Lumières sur la Gaule*, 'a hoard as wonderful and as rich as that of Guarrazar? It is not

impossible.'

But suppose that Alaric did not take the *menorah* and the other treasures of Solomon's Temple from Rome, and that they were in fact returned to Jerusalem by Justinian. If the Persians had really found such legendary booty, surely the fact would have been recorded somewhere in their writings? Perhaps, hidden in some cave in the rock of Jerusalem, or lost beneath a tumbled mass of masonry, it remained undiscovered for centuries.

Jerusalem fell to the Crusaders in 1099, and for nearly a century it remained a Christian city. In 1120 nine knights, under the leadership of Hugues de Payen, vowed to devote themselves to the protection of the Christian shrines, under the name of the Poor Knights of Christ and the Temple of Solomon. They were given quarters in buildings adjacent to the site of the temple, and from that time they have been known as the

Above: one of the golden votive crowns from the treasure of Guarrazar, a Visigothic hoard that remained undiscovered for 11 centuries near Toledo in Spain

Left: the figure of a demon, generally believed to be Baphomet, from the Templar *commanderie* at St Bris-le-Vineux. It is more than superficially reminiscent of the demon in the church of Rennes

Far left: Gaiseric the Vandal sacked Rome in 455, and is said to have carried off the Temple treasure to North Africa

Knights Templar.

Over the next century, the Templars grew ever more powerful in Jerusalem and in the Holy Land. They owed allegiance to none but their Order, and the Grand Master counted himself as important as any king. Their headquarters was the al-Aqsa mosque, built by the Arabs within the precincts of the temple, and they used its crypt as stables – the 'Stables of Solomon'. They were driven from Jerusalem by Saladin in 1187, but they returned between the years 1229 and 1244. And in all the countries of western Europe they established themselves, rich and powerful and inviolate. They ruled large estates and collected tribute, much of which they transported to the Levant, setting up a chain of treasure houses and acting as bankers for non-members of the society.

Guardians of the mystery?

Did all the secrets of the Templars die with them? No, says tradition. Their rites of initiation are reputed to have been adopted by the Freemasons, whose higher degrees include the Grand Priory of Knights Templars. Another Masonic degree, currently 18th in the 'Ancient and Accepted Rite', is that of the Rose Croix, which first made its appearance in France in the 1750s. In England in 1865 a group of Freemasons founded the Societas Rosicruciana in Anglia, and out of this in 1887 grew the Hermetic Order of the Golden Dawn. One of the three Chiefs of the Golden Dawn was S. L. (MacGregor) Mathers, who subsequently introduced the Order of the Rose of Ruby and Cross of Gold (RR et AC). Mathers moved to Paris in 1891, and there he instituted the 'Ahathor' temple of the Golden Dawn, one of whose members was Jules Bois.

At the same time, several so-called 'Rosicrucian' movements were founded in France: the two most prominent were Stanislas de Guaita's Ordre Kabbalistique de la Rose-Croix, and l'ordre de la Rose-Croix, du Temple et du Graal, formed by Joséphin (Sar) Péladan and the Comte de Rochefoucauld. According to a work entitled *Levitikon*, published early in the 19th century in France, the Knights Templar survived their destruction by Philippe IV, and members claiming a direct descent of initiation can be found in several European countries at the present day.

And there is also the shadowy, unacknowledged, order of Le Prieuré de Sion. . . .

Right: Jacques de Molay, the Grand Master of the Templars when the Order was destroyed in the years 1307–11. Under torture, de Molay confessed to denying Christ and worshipping the demon Baphomet

Far right: at the entrance to the tiny village of Rennes-le-Château, a crude hand-painted sign announces 'Excavations forbidden'. With permission, certain excavations were made in 1964, but they revealed very little of interest other than a skull with a slot ritually cut into it – presumably a relic of the time when Rennes was a Visigothic city

over southern Europe, it could have been buried in the foundations or smuggled out to some other hiding-place. And those who knew where it had been hidden took the secret with them to the grave. And let us not forget that the Cathars too had a very valuable treasure.

So, one way or another, the trail leads back to the Razès region and its ancient capital, Rennes-le-Château. Whether the Visigoths stored the sacred treasure of Jerusalem there when they returned it from Ravenna, or whether Bertrand de Blanchefort discovered it deep in the ruins of Solomon's Temple and carried it back to France – whatever the truth, we are unlikely to learn it now, a thousand years or more later.

Did Bérenger Saunière find an ancient hoard of gold and appropriate it to himself? Or did he uncover some other secret that required his silence to be bought? Or was he, perhaps, the unwitting tool of a different, greater, conspiracy?.

But in 1307, jealous of the power and wealth of the Templars, Philip IV of France accused the Order of heresy, and within four years they had been destroyed. In France 54 went to the stake, many hundreds were imprisoned for life, and all their estates were taken from them.

Exactly what form the Templar heresy took has been debated for centuries. The Grand Master, Jacques de Molay, confessed under torture to denying Christ, spitting on the crucifix, and worshipping an idol known as Baphomet, but little is known of the alleged secret rituals practised by initiates. What seems likely, however, is that during their centuries in the Levant the Christianity of the Templars had been infected by some kind of dualism very similar to that professed by the Cathars. And 150 years before, the first Grand Master of the Templars to be granted that title 'by the Grace of God' had been Bertrand de Blanchefort, whose lands lay at the heart of the Catharist regions, and surrounded Rennes-le-Château.

Much of the treasure of the Templars was never surrendered. Stored in great castles all

Mystery at the centre of the golden web

WHEN BÉRENGER SAUNIÈRE spent so many nights in the cemetery of Rennes-le-Château erasing the inscriptions on the two memorial stones from the grave of Marie de Negri d'Ables, he did not realise that they had already been copied: one in the *Bulletin de la société des études scientifiques de l'Aude*, the other in a rare book by Eugène Stublein, *Pierres gravées du Languedoc*.

The first stone, which stood upright at the head of the grave, was subsequently lost and has not been found. Even for a period when monumental masons were notoriously careless about their work the tablet is remarkable for its errors and for its cavalier wordbreaks. All authorities are agreed that the gravestone is probably the work of the then abbé of Rennes-le-Château, Antoine Bigou.

The second stone, which lay horizontally at the foot of the first, survives, now blank, as the cover for an ossuary in the north-west corner of the cemetery. It was carved with a number of enigmatic phrases and devices, among them a monogrammatic device that also appears on one of the manuscripts discovered by Saunière.

One of the phrases is easily recognised. Carved in two parts, down each side of the stone, in Greek characters, it is the well-known Latin motto, *Et in Arcadia ego*. This famous phrase, which has been adopted by many artists and writers, has been variously understood; but its true translation is 'I am also in Arcadia'. It implies that, even in the legendary paradise of the Greek shepherds, death is still present.

One of the reproductions of paintings in the Louvre that Bérenger Saunière brought back with him from Paris was of Nicolas Poussin's *The shepherds of Arcadia*, which was painted some time between 1635 and 1650. This shows three classical shepherds and a shepherdess before a bulky tomb; one of the shepherds is tracing with his finger the words carved upon the face of the tomb: 'Et in Arcadia ego'. And less than 6 miles (10 kilometres) from Rennes-le-Château, on a rocky mount beside the road, one can find the very tomb. It has been covered with a thin layer of cement, so that any inscription can no longer be seen but its shape is unmistakable, and even certain mountain prominences on the skyline can be identified in the Poussin painting. And this 'Arcadian' tomb lies within the parish boundaries of the village of Arques – pronounced, in the local dialect, Arkess.

What else can we discover from the slab in

Far from Paris, even farther from Rome, an obscure roadside monument near Rennes-le-Château is the model for a painting, executed in Italy by Poussin, that now hangs in the Louvre. This chapter investigates the riddles connecting the Abbé Saunière with tales of buried treasure and knightly orders

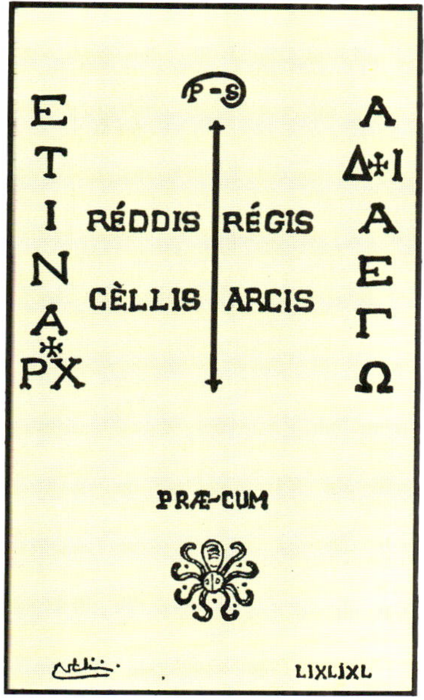

A tale of three tombs.
Above: the slab from the grave of Marie de Negri d'Ables, with the motto *Et in Arcadia ego* inscribed in Greek characters

Left: the most famous portrayal of the tomb in Arcadia, the painting by Nicolas Poussin in the Louvre

Above left: apparently the model for the tomb in Poussin's painting – although a recent covering of cement obscures any former inscription. This enigmatic monument stands on a rocky mount not far from Rennes-le-Château, in the parish of Arques

question? The monogram 'P-S' is the same as on one of the manuscripts, and will be referred to later. The Latin form *Prae-cum* occurs on a third stone discovered in the vicinity of Rennes-le-Château. The central phrase on the slab, which is in crude Latin, can be read either horizontally as 'Reddis Regis, Cellis Arcis' or vertically as 'Reddis Cellis . . . Regis Arcis'. Translation of this rather crude Latin is difficult, but consider the meaning of the individual words:

Reddis: either 'of Rhedae', that is, 'of Rennes' or 'who restoreth'
Regis: 'of the king'
Cellis: 'in a concealed place, or shrine'
Arcis: 'enclosed, in safe keeping'

But there is little doubt about the meaning of the spider engraved on the slab.

The French for spider is *araignée*, which in the local dialect is frequently pronounced 'arenn': this is in fact a hieroglyph for *à Rennes*, 'at (or of) Rennes'. The same device appears in a painting of the Descent from the Cross in the church of Rennes-les-Bains, where the crown of thorns has been given the appearance of a gigantic spider. This painting was presented to the church by the marquis Paul-François-Vincent de Fleury de Blanchefort, son-in-law of Marie de Negri d'Ables and Francis d'Hautpoul.

A mystery surrounds the inheritance of the family d'Hautpoul. In 1644, François-Pierre d'Hautpoul, baron of Rennes, made his will and attached to it documents supporting the family's claim to the title over 600 years. The will and the documents were lost for 130 years before they were rediscovered among papers in the office of a local notary. But when Pierre d'Hautpoul asked to see the papers he received the reply: 'It would not be prudent on my part to make a will of such great importance public' – before the papers once more vanished. According to the French writer Gerard de Sède, the papers were entrusted to Abbé Bigou, who, on the death of Marie, passed them on to Elisabeth, her unmarried middle daughter. And Elisabeth, throughout her life, refused to reveal their contents.

She claimed that it was 'necessary to decipher and determine what comprised the title of the family and what did not'; and it is rather surprising that, in fact, the title de Blanchefort descended not to the eldest sister Marie, who married her cousin Hautpoul-Félines, but to the youngest, Gabrielle, and so to her husband Paul de Fleury.

To add to the mystery another writer, Maurice Guinguand, claims that in 1884 a local notary approached Abbé Saunière to ask for his assistance in translating some documents in Latin that would give him the title to certain lands that had belonged to Paul-François-Vincent's son, Paul Urbain de Fleury, who had died some 30 years before. A year or so later, this notary suffered a fatal accident while he was out shooting with Saunière.

There are two gravestones to Paul Urbain in the churchyard at Rennes-les-Bains. One reads:

Here lies Paul Urbain de Fleury,
born 3 May 1776
Here lies Paul Urbain de Fleury
died 7 August 1836

and the other reads:

He passed away doing good
The transferred remains of
Paul Urbain, comte de Fleury
died 7 August 1856 aged 60 years

What are we to make of this confusion of dates? Paul Urbain in fact was born, not in 1776 or in 1796, but in 1778. Three years later his grandmother Marie was buried in Rennes-le-Château by Abbé Bigou. In 1792, Bigou refused to take the oath of allegiance to the new French Republic and slipped over the border into Spain, where he died. The Fleury family also went into exile, and did not return to France for some years. By then, the documents had been muddled and lost, and only Marie's gravestones remained.

In the decoration of his church, Saunière made a direct allusion to the Fleury lands. Above the confessional is a large relief representation, in wood and plaster, of Christ on the Mount. The steep little mount is flower-dotted (*fleurie* in French) and the background landscape reveals features of the countryside round Rennes. But what is the golden sack tied with a rope that dominates the foreground?

Several French writers have made play with the significance of the text below this picture: 'Come to me, all ye that are heavy laden, and I will give you rest'. In French, 'you that are heavy laden' is '*vous qui êtes accablés*'; and it is easy to discover the words *été* (summer), *sac à cable* (sack with rope), *blé* (corn, but also slang for treasure).

Riddles of a similar kind have been found

in the inscription to the representation of the Magdalene, which Saunière himself painted on the front face of the altar table. The naive relief shows Mary Magdalene kneeling within a grotto, her fingers interlaced on her lap. Her gaze is fixed upon a crude cross, which appears to have been made from the twigs of an acacia bush. On the ground is a human skull, and beside her an open book. Below is painted a verse from one of the manuscripts:

JÉSU . MEDÉLA . VULNÉRUM + SPES . UNA . POENÍTENTIUM . PER . MAGDA-LENAE . LACRYMAS + PECCATA . NOSTRA . DILUAS .

Loosely translated, this means:

'Jesu, who takest away my pain, a penitent's hope: by virtue of the Magdalene's tears, wash away our sins'

Below left: the panel on the altar table, modelled in relief and painted by Saunière himself. It represents Mary Magdalene in a grotto that closely resembles the one painted by Teniers in his *Temptation of St Antony* (below right)

but Gerard de Sède has drawn attention to the accents on certain of the letters, which would not occur in Latin. He identifies four syllables – JE, DE, NE, NI – and translates them as follows:

> JE = *jais* (jet). There is a disused mine of jet not far from Rennes.
>
> DE = *dé* (dice). A stone in this shape can also be found in the vicinity.
>
> NE = *nez* (nose). At Peyrolles, 3 or 4 miles (5 or 6 kilometres) from Rennes-le-Château, there is another stone in this form.
>
> NI = *nid* (nest). The highest point of the region, the peak of Bugarach, is known as the 'eagle's nest'.

Although ingenious, these identifications are unlikely to be significant: the sites are widely scattered, as much as 6 miles (10 kilometres) from Rennes-le-Château, and in no particular relationship to one another. What is much more significant is the direct association in the picture between the Magdalene, a skull and a grotto.

There are many grottoes and caves round Rennes. In his youth, Saunière would have known an old hermit who lived not far away in the Galamus gorge, in an isolated grotto dedicated to St Antony. Perhaps that is why he brought back from Paris the reproduction of Teniers's St Antony, which figures the saint before a crude altar made from a block of stone on top of which is a human skull. But Teniers's grotto is also strikingly like that in which the Magdalene kneels.

There is a direct link between St Antony and Mary Magdalene that is significant. St Antony is regarded as the first person to organise monastic life by bringing groups of hermits together in communities. Some relics of St Antony were brought to France, and in the 11th century a great cathedral was built to house them. From those who had recovered the relics, and from others drawn to them, the Order of St Antony was formed. It was never as powerful an order as the Templars – and eventually was merged with the other great military order, the Hospitallers of St John – but the Antonines are said to have introduced the cult of St Mary the Egyptian.

This Mary, who lived at the end of the fourth century, had begun life as a harlot in Alexandria. But, inspired by the story of St Antony, she repented and spent the rest of her life alone in the wilderness. She became confused with Mary Magdalene in the legend of the Three Marys, which told how the Magdalene, Mary the wife of Cleophas, and Mary the mother of James had come by boat to the mouth of the Rhône and proceeded to evangelise Provence. The beginnings of this legend are to be found in the 11th century, shortly before the Antonines were established. Mary the Egyptian, equated with Mary Magdalene, was conveniently identified with the cult of the Black Madonna, which had survived all over France in subterranean grottoes dedicated to the ancient Mother Goddess.

So we have the Order of St Antony, Mary Magdalene, and a common connection with grottoes. From this point the thread is more tenuous. The Antonines had maintained

Curious treasure in Rome

Nicolas Poussin (1593/4–1665) spent most of his adult life in Rome. Arriving there in 1624, he suffered a serious breakdown in 1629 – either just after or just before painting the first version of *Et in Arcadia ego* – and returned to Paris for little more than a year in 1640. His first few years in Rome coincided with a great deal of activity in the excavation of ancient sites; and during his illness he was cared for by (and afterwards married) the daughter of Jean Dughet, French cook to the Cavaliere del Pozzo, who was in charge of many of the excavations. Of Dughet it is recorded: 'Near Capo di Bove was found buried a most curious treasure, including a room much decorated with silver; but by the intervention of a spy those that found it gained little by it, for the great part of them were thrown into prison. Only the father-in-law of Monsieur Poussin was exempted, on account that he was cook to the senator.' The current rumour in Rome was that some of the diggers were Goths, who had come from the north on the faith of ancient tradition to seek for treasure.

In 1656 Nicolas Fouquet, who was finance minister to Louis XIV, sent his younger brother Louis to Rome, and recommended him to make contact with Poussin. Shortly afterward, Louis Fouquet wrote to his brother:

'I delivered to M. Poussin the letter that you did him the honour to write to him; he evinced all the joy imaginable. You would not believe, Monsieur, either the pains that he takes in your service, or the affection with which he takes them, nor the worth and integrity that he brings to all things.

'He and I, we have planned certain matters that I could in a little undertake to the end for you, by which M. Poussin could provide you with advantages that kings would have great pains to get from him, and that, after him, perhaps no one in the world could recover in the centuries to come; and, what is more, this could be done without much expense and could even turn to profit, and these are things so hard to discover that no one, no matter who, upon this earth today could have better fortune or even so much . . .'

The secret of the tomb

Poussin's painting *The shepherds of Arcadia* of which there are two versions, present us with some fascinating questions. The first version, which is now in the collection at Chatsworth House in Derbyshire, was inspired by a painting by Guercino executed in 1620, and it seems probable that either Guercino himself or his patron Giulio Rospigliosi, who later became Pope Clement IX, composed the famous phrase 'Et in Arcadia ego'.

In Guercino's painting, two shepherds have come upon a human skull reposing upon a stone block carved with the motto; in Poussin's first version, two shepherds and a shepherdess are reading the inscription on a classically ornamented tomb. The skull is scarcely visible as part of the decoration of the lid of the tomb, and the fourth figure in the painting is a personification of the river Alpheus.

The second version of the painting, the one now in the Louvre, is strikingly different. Gone is the skull, Alpheus has been replaced by a third shepherd, and the poses of the figures are changed. As for the tomb, it has lost all its former elegance and decoration; it is now a near-cubic block of roughly hewn stones, with the characteristic sloping top of the lone tomb outside Arques. It seems impossible that Poussin should have chosen to paint such a monument unless he were familiar with its real-life counterpart. And what can have been his motives for painting this alternative version of a somewhat untypical subject? Certainly it seems to have had a peculiar significance in Poussin's life: when his tomb in Rome was restored by Chateaubriand in 1829, a relief of the Arcadian shepherds was added to it.

close relations with the Teutonic Order of Knights (a crusading force founded in Germany in 1128, and one with which the House of Habsburg seems to have retained some connection) and with the Order of St Lazare, an offshoot of the Hospitallers, that similarly has survived to the present day. And although the Templars were reputedly destroyed in 1307, it was rumoured that some form of succession was maintained. Certainly – following the rise of Freemasonry in France – it was not long before a legendary connection had been claimed between the ancient secrets of the builders of the Temple of Solomon, the Knights Templar, and 'Scottish' Freemasonry. (It was said that the Templars had never been proscribed in Scotland.) In 1792 the Duc de Cossé-Brissac, claiming to be Grand Master of the Templars, was killed by a revolutionary mob. In the 1960s, Pierre de Cossé, Duc de Brissac, became Grand Master of the Order of St Lazare. And four centuries before, the Vicar-General of the Order had been Francis de Fleury.

Once again we find a connection with the ancient chivalric orders of the Crusaders, and one that goes back to the late 16th century. This is significant, because it antedates by 50 years the publication of a little book entitled

Below: the headstone from the grave of Marie de Negri d'Ables. There is a remarkable number of spelling mistakes, and the words are divided in a very arbitrary way. The spacing of these deliberate errors suggests they are intended to provide a clue to the mystery of Rennes-le-Château

```
        ✝
CT GIT NOBLe M
ARIE DE NEGRᵉ
DARLES DAME
DHAUPOUL Dᵉ
BLANCHEFORT
AGEE DE SOIX
ANTE SEPT ANS
DECEDEE LE
XVII JANVIER
MDCOLXXXI
REQUIES CATIN
PACE
```

Fama fraternitatis. This, which was almost certainly fiction, purported to reveal the existence of the order of Rosicrucians. And it is from the publication of the *Fama* that we can date the formation of the Freemasons, who claimed to have access to the secrets of the Rosicrucians – and who soon spread throughout Europe.

Which brings us to the papers that Bérenger Saunière discovered, or claimed to have discovered, in the church at Rennes-le-Château or in the tomb of Marie de Negri d'Ables. Both were 'signed' with monogrammatic devices, one of which also appears on two engraved stones. This can be read as the initials 'P-S' within a curved cartouche, and it also appears as 'B-S' (possibly changed to this form within recent years) above the head of the Devil supporting the holy-water stoup in Saunière's church. The other has been taken to read 'N . . . NOBIS . . .', and recognised as an abbreviation for the phrase 'Non nobis Domine'. But, inverted, it is seen to read 'A . . . SION . . . n'. The English researcher Henry Lincoln has recently proved the existence of yet another masonic order known as – Le Prieuré de Sion.

The priest and the pentagram

Did the Rosicrucians possess an ancient secret handed down to them from the Knights Templar? In the final chapter of this series, the threads of the mystery that surrounds Rennes-le-Château are drawn together. But the central enigma remains . . .

WHEN BÉRENGER SAUNIÈRE arrived in Paris in January 1893, he was plunged into the midst of a quarrel between the Ordre Kabbalistique de la Rose-Croix, headed by Stanislas de Guaita, and the Ordre de la Rose-Croix Catholique, du Temple et du Graal, founded by a flamboyant character called Joséphin Páladan. These two men had once been the best of friends, but neither could tolerate the other's ambition.

Rosicrucianism and the Rose-Croix were far from unfamiliar in France. As early as 1623 the philosopher Descartes was reputed to have been a Rosicrucian, and a document claiming to be the detailed rules of the movement was published in 1777; and in Freemasonry, the eighteenth degree of the 'Scottish' rite is the Knight of the Pelican and the Eagle and Sovereign Prince Rose Croix of Heredom.

But Freemasonry was proscribed at the time of the French Revolution – the Royalists suspected the Freemasons had contributed to the success of the revolution, Republicans were convinced that they had plotted against it – and although Napoleon revived interest in the movement, it was not until the restoration of the monarchy that it really began to flourish again, combined with a growing interest in occult matters. Then, in 1865 in England, a group of masons formed the Societas Rosicruciana in Anglia, and shortly afterward received a visit from the French occultist Eliphas Lévi.

Is there an ancient secret?

The line is a tangled one, and there is little or no evidence to support the extravagant claims that have been made. But if the Templars, or the Antonines, had possessed secret information it could have passed to the Hospitallers, who took over a great deal of Templar property, or it might have been passed from generation to generation of the families that had survived the destruction of the Order. Perhaps the claims of latter-day Rosicrucians to an ancient secret are true; perhaps Freemasonry really holds the key to the Rosicrucian enigma; perhaps the occultists of Paris recognised in the papers that Saunière brought with him a clue to something that had long been missing.

The papers themselves do not appear to be very ancient, but then possibly they are copies of something very much older. Certainly there are some strange features about

Between 1892 and 1896, Josephin Péladan (below) set up a number of *Salons de la Rose-Croix* in Paris. These featured dramatic and musical performances as well as art in 'Rosicrucian' style. The poster reproduced here (left) is particularly interesting for its foreground figures of a Knight Templar, wreathed with laurel, and a papal figure carrying a rolled manuscript

them: like the gravestones, they are thick with what can only be deliberate errors. Gerard de Sède has submitted one of the manuscripts to cryptographic analysis. The process is complicated, involving the identification of 128 marked characters and a keyword; coding the 128 characters twice by means of a device known as a Vigenère square, and then disposing them across six separate chessboards and reading the answer by a succession of knight's moves. The outcome is intriguing, but not very revealing. Translated from the French it reads:

> Shepherdess, no temptation. For Poussin, Teniers, hold the key. Pax DCLXXXI. By the Cross and this horse of God, I reach this daemon guardian at midday. Blue apples.

This is not such a farrago as might at first appear. The decoration of the church does include a repeated blue and white motif that, at a distance, can produce the effect of 'blue apples'. And as for the apparent date for peace in 681: French 'Templar' Freemasons of the 18th century frequently dated the calendar year from a beginning in 1118, which would make 681 into AD 1799.

But it is also worth noting that the date of the death of Marie de Negri d'Ables is given

Mystery of the Rosy Cross

The first stories of the Rosicrucians came in 1614 with the publication of the *Fama fraternitatis*, the *Fame and confession of the fraternity of RC, commonly, of the Rosie Cross*. This told of a certain Brother CRC, who was supposed to have been born in 1378 and died in 1484; he had travelled for many years in Arabia and there learnt all kinds of secrets; and had translated 'the Book M' from Arabic into Latin. On his return to Germany, CRC had founded an order dedicated to healing of the sick and to teaching. In 1604, according to the *Fama*, the uncorrupted body of CRC had been found, holding a parchment of 'the Book T'.

Two years after the publication of the *Fama*, the identity of CRC was revealed in *The chemical wedding of Christian Rosencreutz*, an alchemical allegory. Both books were soon discovered to have been written by Johann Valentin Andreae, a Lutheran thinker and writer, who claimed that they were intended only as a jest, and who protested that he himself was certainly not a Rosicrucian.

(Nevertheless, in his will of 1634, he wrote: 'I shall never leave the true Christian fraternity which, beneath the Cross, smells of the rose . . .')

Nobody admitted to being a member of the Rosicrucian brotherhood, but many people wanted to be. Elias Ashmole, one of the founders of Freemasonry, was one of these; Freemasonry seems to have begun in imitation of what Rosicrucianism was supposed to be, and the connection has been claimed ever since. At various times new movements, all known to be offshoots of masonry, have claimed access to the true secrets of the Rosicrucians. In England, the most successful was the Hermetic Order of the Golden Dawn, which enlisted many well-known intellectuals in its membership, but eventually faded away.

In America, the founder of the Ancient and Mystical Order Rosae Crucis (known as AMORC) was H. Spencer Lewis, a man described by Aleister Crowley as 'one of the charlatans who worked the Rosicrucian racket'.

on her tombstone as MDCOLXXXI. If we leave out the O, which is agreed to be a deliberate error, and M for Marie, we are left once again with DCLXXXI.

However, one can spend many unprofitable hours playing with the meaning of letters, words, phrases and figures. It is more rewarding to look at the 'Daemon guardian' as he crouches by the open door of the church, the sun at midday falling full upon him. This is Asmodeus, who guards the treasure of Solomon; above him stand four angels, and about their feet the motto: 'Par ce signe tu le vaincra'. The phrase translates very well as 'In this sign shalt thou conquer', but more accurately it should be read 'By this sign shalt thou conquer *him*'.

The four angels appear at first sight to have a right hand each in one of the positions for making the sign of the cross, and all French commentators have taken it for granted that this is what is implied. But the topmost angel has her *left* hand upon her breast, while her right hand is held to the top of her head.

The sign referred to here is, of course, the sign of Asmodeus himself, the sign that encompassed the goat-head of Baphomet in the rites of the Templars, the pentagram. It is time to trace this sign upon the land of Rennes-le-Château itself; it is time to climb the Tour Magdala and look out across the wild plateau.

To the north-east, where the thick woods crowd up the steep slope above the river Sals, the stark ruins of the Château de Blanchefort are just visible, on the high ridge above the junction of the Sals and the Blanque. On the morning of 22 July, the feast day of Mary Magdalene, the sun rises directly behind the Blanchefort ruins.

South-eastward, as high on an even steeper ridge above the river Cass-Rats, stand the remains of another Templar castle, known only as the Château des Templiers. Four miles (six kilometres) separate the Château des Templiers from Rennes-le-Château, and from the Château de Blanchefort. The angle between the two bearings is exactly 36 degrees, the internal angle of the pentagram.

On the map we can construct the other points of the five-pointed figure: one is the hilltop beyond the spring known as la Source de la Madeleine, whose summit is marked by two massive menhirs; the fifth is an empty space upon the map. But anybody who takes the winding road eastward from Granès, steadily uphill until the vineyards come to an end, will find a great white convoluted rock, between the curve of the hill and road but just visible from the Tour Magdala.

This is the magic pentagram of Rennes-le-Château, clearly and unambiguously marked at each of its five points. And almost exactly in the middle, a little mound rising in the plateau and prominently visible from the tower, is la Pique, also known as the mount of Coume-Sourde. Here, in 1928, was discovered another engraved stone tablet: it clearly bears the essential elements of a pentagram, the abbreviation *P.S. Praecum* that also appeared upon one of the gravestones of Marie de Negri d'Ables, and a phrase in Latin that translates 'In the middle of the line where M cuts the lesser line'.

But what is M? Could it stand for Mary Magdalene? Or perhaps for Marie de Negri d'Ables? (There is also the fascinating detail

Below: 'By this sign shalt thou conquer him'. Above the stoup in Rennes church, the head of Asmodeus is contained within a pentagram indicated by the hands of a group of angels. According to the 15th-century magical treatise *Lemegeton*, Asmodeus is the guardian of buried treasure

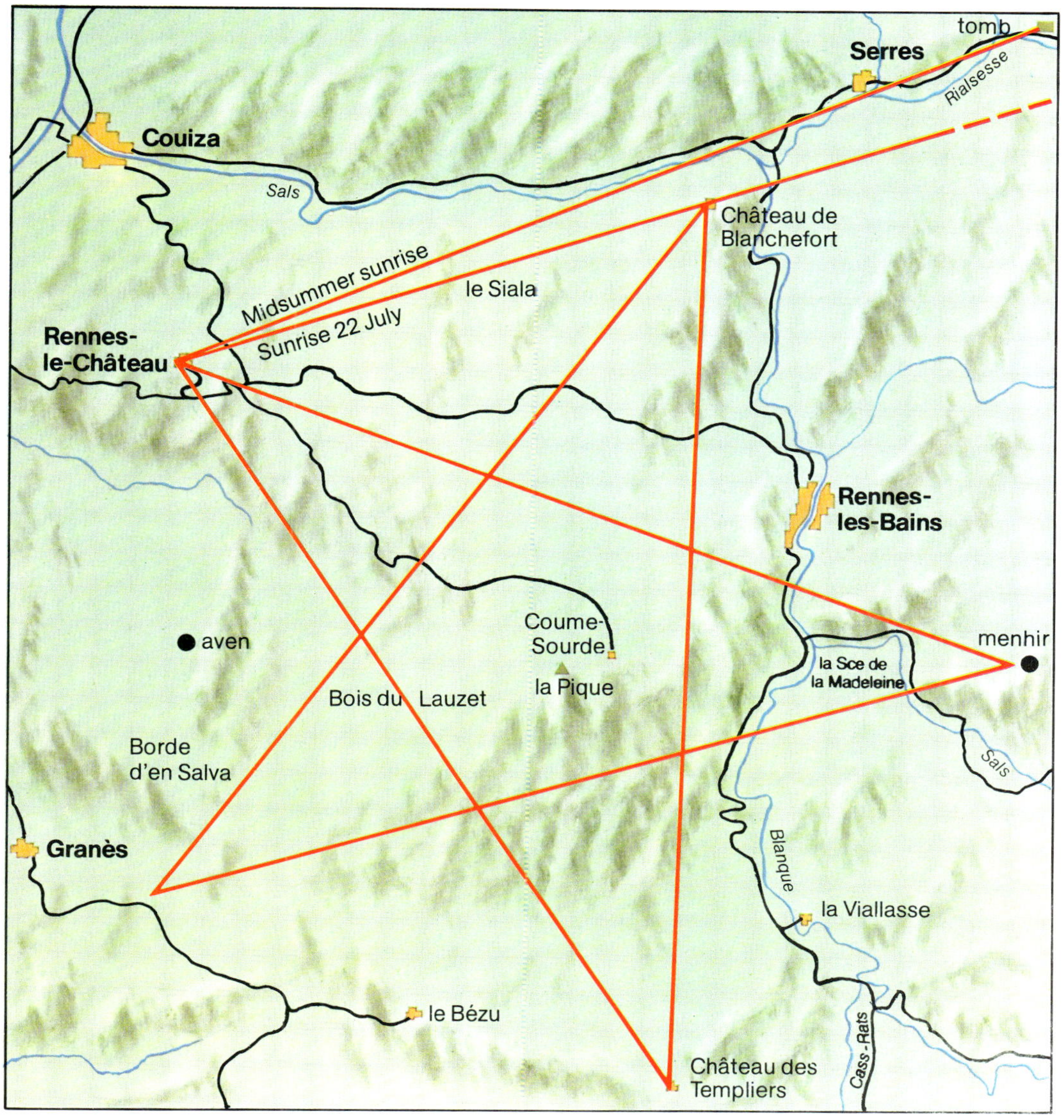

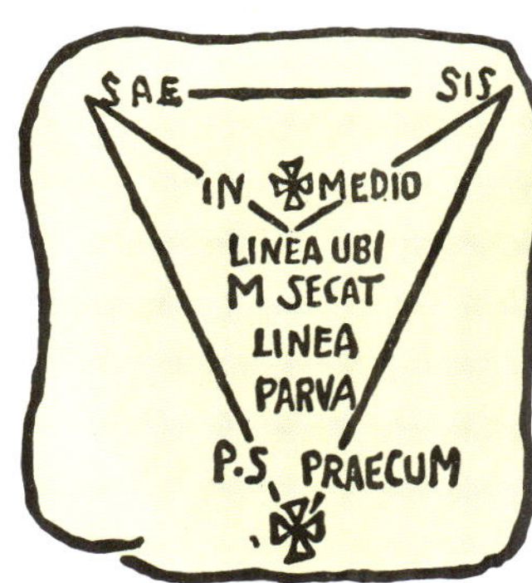

Left: the great pentagram drawn across the plateau of Rennes-le-Château is based upon the positions of the church of St Mary Magdalene and the Château de Blanchefort, and the direction of sunrise on the morning of the feast day of Mary Magdalene, 22 July. At its centre is the mount of Coume-Sourde. Each point of the pentagram is marked by a building or standing stone

Below: At the foot of the fallen rocks of the *aven* (see page 30 and the map left) is a grotto leading down to caves. It is very like the one painted in Rennes church

that the reputed founder of the Rosicrucians, Christian Rosencreutz, gathered all his wisdom from 'the Book ᴍ'.)

If we look again at the gravestone of Marie de Negri d'Ables, and trace lines joining the prominent errors of the inscription, we find that they meet at an angle of 36 degrees, the end of one line being marked by the isolated ᴍ of Marie. But unfortunately we no longer know where this gravestone stood in relation to the grave in Rennes-le-Château cemetery. There is nothing for it but to explore the region on foot, as Bérenger Saunière himself did.

The slab from Coume-Sourde suggests by its design that the 'lesser line' may be the line joining two of the points of the pentagram. The line from Rennes-le-Château to the Château de Blanchefort passes over very uneven ground, through the woods that drop steeply to the Sals valley; and its centre is marked by a steep bare outcrop of rock named le Siala. From Blanchefort to the next point of the pentagram the line plunges down into the valley, through Rennes-les-Bains, and then up and down through the woods

Below: the engraved stone slab discovered on Coume-Sourde in 1928. It very clearly bears the essentials of a pentagram, the abbreviation *P.S. Praecum* – which appears to be part of the sign of the Prieuré de Sion – and the cryptic message: 'In the middle of the line where ᴍ cuts the lesser line'

beyond the town; its centre comes at one of the thermal springs that have fed the baths for many hundred years.

The third connecting line lies well beyond the plateau, cut off from it by the valley of the Blanque, and its centre lies in featureless woodland above the hamlet of la Viallasse. The fourth follows quite closely the high Calmette ridge as far as le Bézu, with its crumbling Templar chapel, which marks the centre point, and then runs close by the road to Granès.

None of these lines is easy to follow: the terrain is very rough and at times impassable, and it is impossible to keep one's landmarks in sight for much of the distance. But from the great white stone outside Granès the line runs straight as a die to the Tour Magdala, which stands, watching on the skyline, far across the almost level plateau.

It is still a tough scramble: skirting the eastern edge of the jagged rocks of the Serre de Lauzet, dropping down through the *maquis* to wade the muddy waters of a narrow stream, then up again past the crumbled ruins of Borde d'en Salva, tracing a narrow track between the fields of oats that unexpectedly cover the floor of a shallow, silent combe, and once more into the *maquis*.

There is no path through the scrub: only wandering tracks made by browsing herds of goats or sheep – but always the Tour Magdala broods in the distance. And then, suddenly, one comes upon it: a crumbling slit in the earth's surface where the rock has broken and fallen into the cavern beneath. This is an *aven*, or swallow-hole, formed through millions of years by the action of water below the surface, and possibly leading to many miles of cave system. It is possible to climb down the tumbled rocks to the mouth of the grotto

Above: the huge white stone that marks the fifth point of the pentagram. From this point the Tour Magdala is clearly visible across the intervening *maquis*. Exactly at the halfway point between the stone and the tower, the ground opens in a narrow *aven*

below which is strikingly like that represented in the painting of Mary Magdalene in Saunière's church. It well fits the description of the chasm in which the shepherd Paris discovered his gold pieces, and it is exactly the kind of cave hinted at by all those who have tried to unravel the riddle of Rennes-le-Château.

Unfortunately it is not possible at the present time to penetrate far into the cave. The floor is silted up with sand, and rocks have fallen to block the passage. Others, no doubt, have been put there by human hands. But this may well be the grotto in which Saunière discovered his treasure.

And there, for the moment, the matter rests. We still do not know, nor are we ever likely to know, exactly what Bérenger Saunière found. The mystery begins with the discovery of the manuscripts, and their connection with the grave of Marie de Negri d'Ables. Only two of the four manuscripts have been photographed and published. Perhaps they were the least important, the others providing more explicit details of the location of a treasure, passed down as hearsay

Left and above right: two of the manuscripts discovered by Saunière. Both are 'signed': that on the left, reversed, reads 'SION'; the other bears the monogram of the Prieuré

from member to member of the Blanchefort family. Perhaps, when Saunière went to Paris, he took with him a piece of a jigsaw puzzle that had eluded others for centuries.

But the missing piece must have been either a further document or the treasure itself, and presumably the tomb at Arques, which was obviously of great significance to Nicolas Poussin, contained some clue – which would account for its having been cemented over. Then the *aven* could well have been the repository of an ancient hoard – of the Visigoths, or the Cathars, or the Templars – of which Saunière (with due supervision) would have been entrusted with the recovery. His journeys about Europe would have been made to collect the various pieces of the reward that was his due, and so, in thankfulness, he would have restored his church with motifs that made enigmatic reference to the source of his new wealth.

The part played by the Prieuré de Sion, the connection with the house of Habsburg, and all the ramifications of this almost unknown organisation – that is another story.

The holy incorruptibles

Of the many miracles associated with the saints none is more mystifying than that of incorruptibility — when their bodies do not decompose after death. BOB RICKARD describes some remarkably well-attested cases

IN DOSTOEVSKY'S *The brothers Karamazov* there is a scandal when the body of a holy ascetic begins to decompose. All over the world there is an instinctive folk belief that holy saints have the power to defy the physical dissolution of their bodies at death. As St Cyril of Jerusalem summed it up, in the fourth century: 'Even when the soul is gone, power and virtue remain in the bodies of the saints because of the righteous souls which have dwelt in them.' Yet even a casual study of the lives of Christian saints reveals that there are a great many of the holy and virtuous who did not receive this mark of 'divine favour', and a number who did were not beatified or canonised. Some of the truly pious even had a horror of this bizarre perpetuation. It is said of the dying St Thérèse of Lisieux (see page 66) that when a novice said she was sure God would preserve her body from corruption, Thérèse replied: 'Oh no. Not that miracle . . .' God granted her wish.

There has been remarkably little study of this strange subject despite the high quality of the proofs demanded by the Congregation for the Causes of Saints in the process of canonisation. And the Church records

Above: the faithful flock to touch the magnificent reliquary in the cathedral at Goa, India, that holds the body of St Francis Xavier. The great Catholic missionary died in 1552 and was immediately buried in quicklime. Yet his body was not destroyed and even today remains astonishingly lifelike

Above right: priests in Madrid venerate one of St Francis Xavier's well-preserved arms. Frequently parts of the incorruptibles have been removed — in an act known as 'translation' — to be used as holy relics

demand serious consideration because exhumations and examinations have nearly always been carried out before many witnesses, including where possible doctors and medical specialists. It seems astonishing that so well-documented a fact as the incorruption of certain persons should have escaped medical scrutiny for so long.

Father Herbert Thurston, the subject's first historian (writing in the late 19th century), describes six types of phenomena associated with cases of incorruption (not all of which may occur in the same case): very often a persistent fragrance is reported emanating from the body; an absence of rigor mortis; absence of putrefaction; sometimes there is a bleeding (from stigmata or wounds suffered in martyrdom, for example) long after death; in a few cases the body is felt to be warm long after death: even more rarely there is some kind of ritualised movement of the limbs (for example, giving a blessing) that cannot be accounted for by mere contraction of muscles. To this we may add another group of phenomena frequently encountered in cases of incorruption: often the secret or long-forgotten burial place of the saint is revealed to his discoverers by a dream or vision; sometimes their first interment is marked by unusual phenomena, like the strange lights that played around the grave of St Charbel Makhlouf; long-dead bodies, or their remaining parts, frequently exude a fragrant clear oil in great quantities, whose origin and composition is a mystery, as in the case of St Walburga who died in AD 779 and from whose bones, to this day, there distils an oil; finally, to this exudation, as well as to the relics of their bodies, blood and clothing, are attributed great powers of healing, the success of which has been established at many shrines by medical case histories.

The Cruz file

The only other work of any note on incorruption is that of a New Orleans housewife, Joan Cruz, who over many years patiently extended the lists of incorrupt saints begun by Father Thurston, by going through all the generally available ecclesiastical biographies. Her book, *The incorruptibles* (published in 1977), contains 102 such cases approved by the Congregation for the Causes of Saints of the Catholic Church. There may be a great many others, adds Cruz, lying undiscovered in their graves, or whose details are hidden in the secret archives of the Vatican. Even such a prodigious sweep through the hagiographical literature failed to turn up a study of incorruption by any physician, eminent or otherwise, other than the statements of those doctors who attended specific post-mortem examinations. The following case is typical. Blessed Maria Anna Ladroni died in Madrid in 1624. One hundred and seven years later she was examined for the second time by ecclesiastical authorities during the process

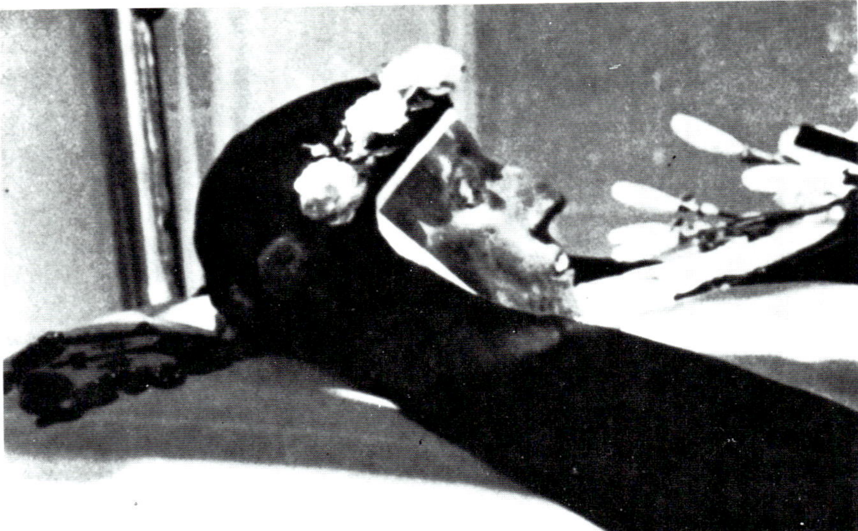

Above: St Teresa Margaret, who died in 1770, as she appears today in her glass coffin in Florence, Italy. Although a little dried and discoloured, her body shows no sign of putrefaction. This is all the more remarkable for she died of a gangrenous condition, her corpse appearing rigid, swollen and purple just after her death. But two days later she had assumed the radiant beauty and fragrance of a true incorruptible

Below: St Bernadette of Lourdes, who looks as fresh and lifelike as when she lay dying in 1879. Her face is, however, now covered with a thin layer of wax to prevent discolouration

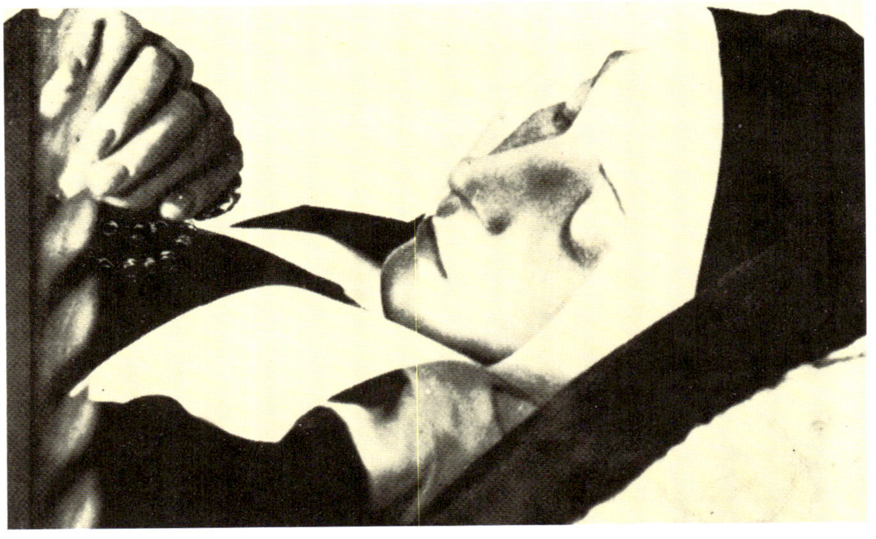

of her beatification. According to her official biography:

Not less than eleven professors of medicine and surgery, all of them among the first and most famous in the city and court of Madrid, took part in the proceedings and made deposition as witnesses. They took out their instruments and made some long and deep incisions in the fleshy parts, others laid open the breast, others scrutinized the cavities thus exposed to view, others explored any orifice by which it might have been possible to introduce preservatives against putrefaction. In fact their united efforts resulted in what was . . . an absolute dissection of this innocent body . . . The interior organs, the viscera and the fleshy tissues were all of them entire, sound, moist and resilient. The fluid which was observed to exude from the body impregnated all the interior and all the substance of the flesh. The deeper the incisions which were made, the sweeter was the fragrance which was emitted from them . . .

One of the astonishing aspects of incorruption is not that it happens at all, but that it frequently happens to bodies under conditions that would encourage the normal processes of disintegration, including that of death caused by disease, and burial in close proximity to other bodies that decomposed normally. Some, like St Charbel, St Catherine of Bologna, and St Pacifico of San Severino, had been consigned to the bare earth without any ill effect, except perhaps some minor distortion by the pressure of the earth. Others survived – if one may use the word – burial in such damp conditions that their clothes rotted off their intact bodies, as in the case of St Teresa of Avila and St Catherine of Genoa. The coffin of St Catherine of Siena (who died in 1380) was actually left exposed to the rain for some time before being brought indoors. And when the body of the visionary St Catherine Labouré was exhumed in Paris in 1933, 56 years after her death, her body was incorrupt despite the moisture that had attacked her triple coffin.

A number of the incorruptibles had been stigmatics during life, and in some cases their mysterious wounds persisted beyond the grave. St Catherine of Siena believed she bore the marks of Christ's Passion invisibly, and on her death the wounds appeared on her hands, feet and side. When her body was examined and parts detached as separate relics – an act called a 'translation' – one such mark was still visible on her perfect left foot in 1597 (217 years after her death). In the case of Blessed Osanna of Mantua (who died in 1505), whose intact body is still displayed in the cathedral at Mantua three times a year, her stigmata became even more pronounced than they had been in life. At the exposition in 1965, her body was described as dried, browned and shrunken, but without any sign of corruption.

One of the most modern cases is that of St Charbel Makhlouf, who died at the Hermitage of St Peter and St Paul at the St Maroun monastery in Annaya, Lebanon, in 1898. In accordance with the custom of his order, like many of the incorrupt, he was buried without a coffin. For many weeks strange lights were seen around his grave – as

in the case of St John of the Cross, who died in 1591 and who was still flexible and moist (but slightly discoloured) at the last public exposition at Segovia, Spain, in 1955. Because of the unusual lights an exhumation was ordered by the monastery's superiors, and the common grave was opened 45 days later.

St Charbel's body was perfectly intact despite the rain and floods that had made the grave a pit of mud and water. The body was washed and reclothed and placed in a wooden coffin in the monastery chapel. In a short time an oily liquid – said to be blood and perspiration, and smelling of fresh blood – seeped from its pores, so copiously that the clothing had to be changed twice a week. Many cures were attributed to pieces of the soaked cloth. There the body remained until 1927, when, after a medical examination, the

Left: painting by Sodoma showing the religious ecstasy of the stigmatic St Catherine of Siena. During her life she believed she bore invisible marks of Christ's suffering, and felt great pain; after her death in 1380 the marks became clearly visible, remaining so for over 200 years

Overleaf: one of the most revered of all incorruptibles is the Curé of Ars (a village in France) who died in 1859 and was canonised in 1925 (and later named patron saint of parish priests). Shortly after his death he was discovered to be incorrupt (top) and his body put on public display in the Basilica in Ars. Although his face has been covered with his waxen death mask to prevent discolouration, his body is said to remain miraculously preserved (bottom)

Left: an artist's impression of St Charbel Makhlouf as he appeared towards the end of his life. The Lebanese hermit died in 1898 at the age of 70; some months later dazzling lights were seen around his tomb in the cemetery of Annaya. Taking them to be a sign of divine favour, the monks exhumed his body and found it to be completely incorrupt and exuding what appeared to be a mixture of fresh blood and sweat. Although his body has been inspected annually since 1950, this mysterious oozing shows no signs of stopping. Many miraculous cures have been ascribed to holy relics associated with him – such as pieces of cloth soaked in the liquid – and the incorrupt hermit was declared a saint in 1977

body was placed in a wood-lined zinc coffin, with reports from doctors and witnesses sealed in a zinc tube at its feet, and bricked into the monastery wall. Twenty-three years later, in 1950, pilgrims to the shrine noticed a liquid oozing through the wall, and the tomb was opened. Once again, in the presence of ecclesiastical and medical authorities, St Charbel was found to be completely lifelike and flexible. His partly rotted clothing was soaked in the oily fluid (much of which had solidified in the coffin). The zinc tube was badly corroded, but the saint was free of any corruption. Every year since then his tomb has been opened and the body carefully examined. And each time it seems fresh and intact, and the oily exudation, which collects to a depth of about 3 inches (8 centimetres), is drained off for distribution as a healing cure.

A number of the early incorruptibles were English saints, perhaps the most famous being the popular Anglo-Saxon foundress of Ely Monastery, St Etheldreda, who died in AD 679. Sixteen years later her sister, St Sexburga, who had succeeded her as abbess of Ely, exhumed Etheldreda's remains to entomb them in the church. One of the witnesses, a doctor called Cynefrid – who had removed a tumour from Etheldreda's jaw only three days before she died – was interviewed by no less a person than the Venerable Bede, who recorded the statement in his *Ecclesiastical history*:

> And when so many years after her bones were to be taken out of the grave, a pavilion being spread over it, all the

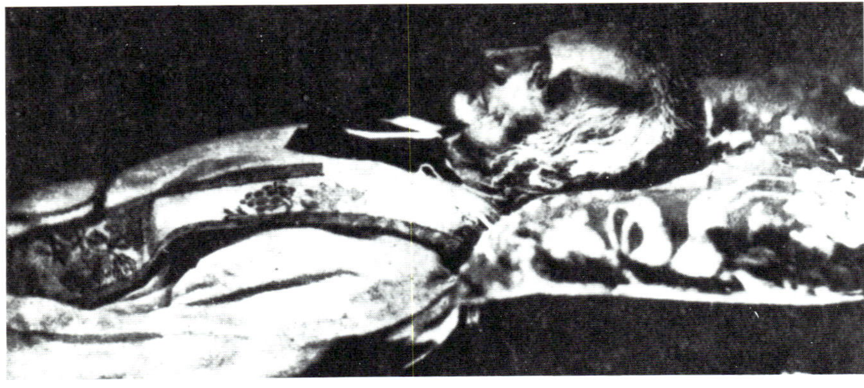

marble sarcophagus and, in front of a large crowd, its lid was prised off to reveal St Cecilia's body in her dying position and still totally incorrupt after almost 1500 years. The body – with the neck wound plainly visible – went on view for a month before its reinstatement beneath the altar in a special casket commissioned by Pope Clement VIII.

An even more bizarre case, which defies all the normal expectations, is the martyrdom of the Polish saint, Andrew Bobola, at the hands of the Cossacks in 1657. After a cruel beating he was dragged by horses from one town to another, partly flayed, and had parts of his face and limbs torn away before being dispatched by a sabre. He was hastily buried in a churchyard at Pinsk, during a hot summer, in moist ground and in the midst of many other corpses whose bodies had decayed normally. Forty years later his body was discovered intact (apart from his wounds), and has since been subjected to many medical examinations. In 1917 it was on exhibition, still pliable and well-preserved. In 1922, Red Army troops, hearing of the legend of St Andrew's preservation, surrounded the church at Pinsk and broke open his tomb. After dragging out the body and presumably satisfying their curiosity, they left it on the floor. It was taken

congregation of brothers were on the one side, and of sisters on the other, and the abbess, with a few, being gone to take up and wash the bones, on a sudden we heard the abbess within loudly cry out . . . Not long after they called me in, opening the door of the pavilion, where I found the body of the holy virgin taken out of the grave and laid on a bed, as if it had been asleep.

To his astonishment Cynefrid noticed that in place of the great wound in her jaw, there was now 'only an extraordinarily slender scar'. Even the clothes in which she was buried were intact. St Etheldreda's new resting place became one of the most famous shrines in England, until Henry VIII ordered the church destroyed and its relics scattered.

A bizarre example of incorruption is afforded by one of the oldest cases, that of St Cecilia, of a noble Roman family, and martyred in AD 177. An inexperienced executioner bungled her beheading, and she lay for three days dying on the floor of her family home, her hands crossed in prayer, her face to the floor and her neck half-severed. Her body was dressed in rich robes, and placed in the catacomb of St Callistus in the exact position in which she died. In AD 822, her secret burial place was revealed in a vision to Pope Pascal I, who placed her body beneath the altar of the basilica dedicated to her name. It was rediscovered during restoration work on the basilica 777 years later. From reliable eyewitness testimony we know that, on 20 October 1599, the original cypress coffin was found in a good condition inside a

A statue of the early Christian martyr St Cecilia of Rome, which lies above her remains. The statue is widely believed to be an exact representation of her body as it was found 1500 years after her martyrdom in AD 177: her beheading was incomplete (as the neck wound clearly shows), and she was buried in the position in which she had lain, for three days, dying. In October 1599 her coffin was opened and her body discovered to be undisturbed and whole

to Moscow and returned years later only after a plea by Pope Pius XI. The relic now resides in the church in Warsaw that bears his name.

Many of the incorruptibles met deaths either by violence or by the usual selection of diseases that afflict more ordinary mortals. The presence of livid wounds (as in the case of St Andrew Bobola) or the bacteriological seeds of putrefaction (as in cancerous conditions) should have hastened corruption. But somehow these special bodies did not decay. Many people might be inclined to dismiss such stories as the product of an intense religious belief, spread by the faithful of a less sceptical age. But incorrupt bodies have been authenticated in our own day.

A bizarre preservation

Above: the head of a Tollund man, dating from the Danish Iron Age. A sacrificial victim, killed by strangulation, he has been perfectly preserved – if extremely discoloured – by the natural chemical processes of the bog into which he was thrown

The phenomenon of dead bodies that do not decay may often be explained in natural terms but, as this chapter points out, there remain many cases of incorruptibility that defy rational explanation

THE RECORDS OF THE SAINTS of the Catholic Church contain the greatest concentration of incorruptibles – bodies of mystics who, in the words of the Church historian Father Thurston, have resisted 'the horror of the tomb'. However, Roman Catholics have no monopoly of bodies that defy decay: they are met with in every branch of the Christian Church, and also among the other religions. For example, descriptions strikingly similar to the Catholic accounts are to be found in the Chinese annals known as *The lives of the Buddhist saints*.

The story of Hui Neng, one of the best known of the Ch'an (or Zen) patriarchs, particularly echoes in some respects the violation of the body of St Andrew Bobola by Red Army troops (see opposite page). Hui Neng died in AD 712 and was buried in the Kuo-en monastery where he had taught, in Kwantung province. During the fall of the Sung Dynasty, in 1276, Mongol troops dragged out his body to see for themselves his rumoured miraculous preservation. After 564 years the Zen master's skin was still flexible and glossy, and there was no sign of collapsing or shrinking. The desecrators then cut open the body to find the heart and liver in a perfect condition. They were impressed enough to depart immediately without further sacrilege.

A 'divine favour'

The phenomenon occurs today, as the following examples drawn from outside the specific Catholic context clearly prove. In 1977, a family grave in Espartinas, Spain, was opened to inter the body of a local man. The sexton and his helpers were shocked to find that the body of the man's son was still intact after 40 years. The boy, José Garcia Moreno, died in 1937 of meningitis at the age of 11, and the family deny that he was embalmed. Soon the whole village had viewed the body in its rotting grave-clothes – and, believing the boy must have been a saint to be so 'favoured', have begun to petition Rome for his canonisation. However, as Father Thurston points out, phenomena such as stigmata, visions, levitation or incorruption are less important to the Congregation for the Causes of Saints in the recognition of a saint than a life of piety and virtue.

One case has come to light with only minimal religious colouring. In 1644, a beautiful Hungarian countess, Zofia Bosniakova, died at the age of 35, having been married twice and bearing one son. Her first husband died within a year of her marriage at 17, and the brawling promiscuous ways of her second husband – Franco Wesselenyi, a renowned swordsman and diplomat – made her retreat into a simple, pious and private life in Strečno Castle, in northern Slovakia. During renovations of the castle in 1689 her coffin was opened to reveal her flawless beauty. The local history, which may not be entirely reliable, says 'The Lady of Strečno', although not beatified, lies in state today in a

Below: the remains of Wilhelm Von Ellenborgen who died in Philadelphia in 1792. Most of his body has turned into *adipocere*, a soap-like substance thought to be created by the nearby ground water

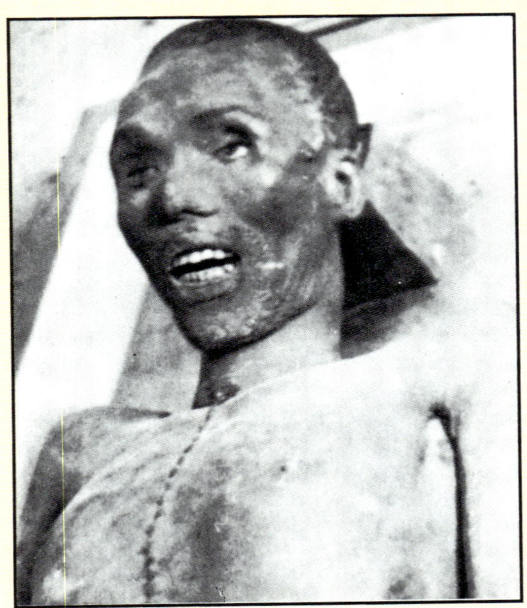

A legend in the making

At the end of 1980 in the ancient city of Kano in northern Nigeria, state troops were called in to quell a riot caused by the followers of a heretical Muslim cult, led by the self-styled prophet Muhammadu Marwa (or Maitatsine, as he was also known). Marwa established his headquarters in Kano during the 1960s and since then he is said to have attracted some 10,000 followers. Tension between his sect and the orthodox Muslims exploded into riot in December 1980, during which as many as 8000 people were killed, including Marwa.

At first Marwa was buried in the bare earth in a shallow grave, but three weeks later the Governor gave orders that his body be exhumed and placed on ice at the city mortuary (left). Rumour soon spread among the people of Kano that Marwa's body was miraculously incorruptible.

church in Teplice-Sanov, Czechoslovakia, in a robe she made herself. She is still beautiful after 336 years.

There is another case that gives the usual pious morality of these stories a new twist. It concerns the body of a German knight, called Christian Kahlbutz, who sounds as if he might have been the model for Countess Zofia's second husband. Kahlbutz bravely acquitted himself in 1675, defending his homeland of Brandenburg against the Swedish invaders. But domestically he was a tyrant, who, among other abuses, insisted on his *droit de seigneur* (the feudal custom that allowed a lord to usurp a peasant bridegroom's conjugal rights on the wedding night). Besides his own 11 children, it seems he fathered more than 30 on local girls. It was when one of them refused his advances that he revenged himself by killing her fiancé. The girl took him to court, but he escaped justice because of his social position and by swearing solemnly: 'If I was the murderer, then shall the good Lord never let my body rot.' He died in 1702, and it was not until over 90 years later, when the new lords of the manor were renovating the local church, that his incorrupt body was found in its coffin, and the crime that everyone believed he committed was openly confirmed.

No doubt large parts of this story are a curious mixture of folklore and the opportunism of local moralists, but the unusual preservation of the knight's body seems a verifiable fact. During the 1936 Berlin Olympic Games, coachloads of visitors were taken to the village of Kampehl (now in East Germany) to see the browned and desiccated body in its open coffin. So many people were writing graffiti on the shroud, which had remained intact since his burial, that a glass top had to be placed over the coffin. In 1895, Rudolf Virchow, a well-known pathologist,

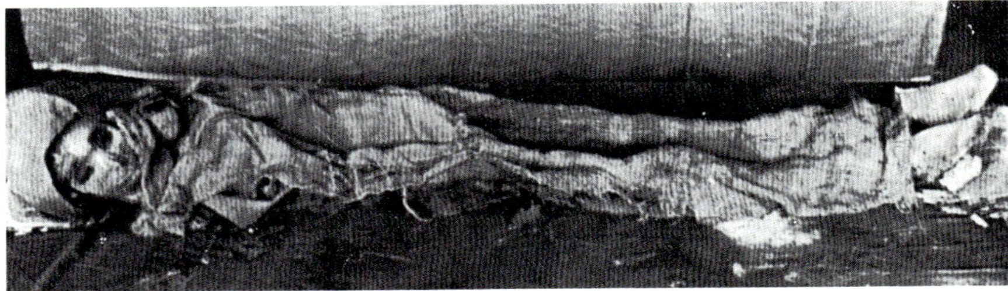

Top: the 'young lady of Loulan' was unearthed in China's remote Xinjiang province in 1981. Experts claim that this 6470-year-old mummy is the oldest in the world

Above: Julia Buccola Petta, when her body was exhumed in 1927 – six years after her death. Her lifelike preservation was believed to be miraculous; this photograph was taken to be made into the plaque that now adorns her grave in Mount Carmel Cemetery, Hillside, Illinois

had carried out an autopsy. He failed to find any trace of embalming preservatives, and confirmed that the internal organs and the general condition of the body were remarkably good. At least one other medical expedition set out from Berlin to investigate and test various alternative theories, but left the riddle as intact as the body.

So what are the hypotheses most frequently put forward as alternatives to the idea of a miracle? To begin with, there are various kinds of embalming, but they can safely be ignored since in most of the fully authenticated cases it is clear from medical examination that no preservatives had been used and none of the viscera removed as is essential in embalming. Some bodies, however, like that of St Francis Xavier, did have internal organs removed for use as holy relics; the incorruptible state was discovered only when the tomb was first opened to take relics.

Joan Cruz, author of *The incorruptibles*, outlined three categories of preserved bodies. Those preserved deliberately; the accidentally or naturally preserved; and the true incorruptibles. Those that fit into the second category show effects no less wonderful for having a mundane explanation. Father Thurston and Cruz cite many places that have reputations for preserving human bodies (and not always in a mummified form). Cruz mentions the discovery of a natural mummy in a mountain cave in Chile in 1954, thought to be the body of a boy who had been drugged and left there to freeze as a sacrifice about 500 years previously. Bodies of Iron Age people have been found perfectly preserved in peat bogs in Denmark, Ireland and Scotland, but they are greatly discoloured by natural chemical processes. Preservations in alcohol, formaldehyde, honey, rum, sand, salt, and many other unusual compounds – including guano – have been known, but such bodies are not true incorruptibles.

Certain sites have been deliberately chosen as burial grounds because their natural conditions delayed the onset or acceleration of decomposition. The Capuchin catacombs of Palermo and Malta are famous for their gruesome specimens, of which one 19th-century travel writer wrote: 'They are all dressed in the clothes they usually wore . . . the skin and muscles become as dry and hard as a piece of stockfish, and though many of them have been here upwards of two

A grisly display of dead Capuchin monks, hanging like so many broken dolls in the catacombs in Palermo, Sicily. Most bodies left exposed to the air decay approximately eight times faster than those that are buried – but the air in these catacombs has the peculiar property of drying out the bodies and turning them into natural mummies

hundred and fifty years, yet none are reduced to skeletons.' In the 18th century burial in the lead-lined crypt of the cathedral at Bremen became fashionable among the German aristocracy, after the discovery of the astonishingly well-preserved body of a workman who had met with a fatal accident down there several years earlier and had never been found.

The vaults under St Michan's Church in Dublin have similar qualities. A survey of the church in 1901 mentions the striking example of 'a pathetic baby corpse, from whose plump wrists still hang the faded white ribbons of its funeral', with the date 1679 on the coffin. The preservative effect is believed to be caused by the extreme dryness of the air and its freedom from dust – conditions that also prevail in the necropolis at Kiev, Russia, in which a large number of withered bodies lie in their open coffins (now covered with glass). As in the case of the German knight, radiation was suggested as the preserving agent of the 250-year-old desiccated bodies found in the Wasserburg Somersdorf Castle, at Mittelfranken, also in Germany. Even though tiny amounts of radiation have been detected in the castle tombs, we cannot generalise from this to explain all odd mummifications, nor the truly intact bodies. At each of the above sites the bodies have finally become shrivelled, horribly distorted and extremely rigid. These conditions, as Joan Cruz points out, simply do not apply to the true cases, which 'are quite moist and flexible, even after the passage of centuries.'

Preserved – as soap

A further consideration is the curious natural process known as *saponification*. In this, as the name suggests, the body tissues are turned into an ammoniacal soap beneath a toughened outer skin. This soap-like substance is called 'adipocere' (from the Latin *adeps* for fat, and *cera* meaning wax) – or *gras de cadavre* (French, meaning 'corpse fat') – and is caused by burial in damp soil in the proximity of putrefaction. Why it develops in some cases and not others is unknown. Monsieur Thouret, who was commissioned to clear the cemetery of the Church of the Holy Innocents in Paris, in 1785, found that many bodies had converted to adipocere:

> The bodies themselves, having lost nothing of their bulk, and appearing to be wrapped in their shrouds, like so many larvae, had, to all seeming, suffered no decay. On tearing apart the grave-clothes which enveloped them, the only change one noticed consisted in this, that they had been converted into a flabby mass or substance the whiteness of which stood out the more clearly in contrast to the blackness in which they lay.

Their plumpness, eyes and hair were all unimpaired after five years or more.

Saponification is unusual but not rare –

there is a saponified soldier from the United States Civil War period in the Smithsonian Museum, Washington – and occurrences among the religious have not caused any undue excitement; although, when medical knowledge was more primitive, it seems likely that a few cases of alleged incorruption might be attributed to adipocere. In support of this idea he describes the exhumation of Blessed Marie de Sainte-Euphrasie Pelletier, who died in 1868. Thirty-five years later her lead coffin was opened to, reveal the recognisable features of the foundress of the Good Shepherd Nuns. 'The mouth was slightly open, the eyes shut, the eyelashes intact,' wrote one examining doctor. Without unclothing the body, he was 'able to ascertain that the chest, the abdomen, the thighs and the legs were covered with a skin like that of a mummy, under which was a mass of *gras de cadavre*, resulting from the saponification of the tissues underneath.' A second doctor added: 'I may say that, in general, the skin, mummy-like, hard to the touch, and resonant when struck by a metal instrument,

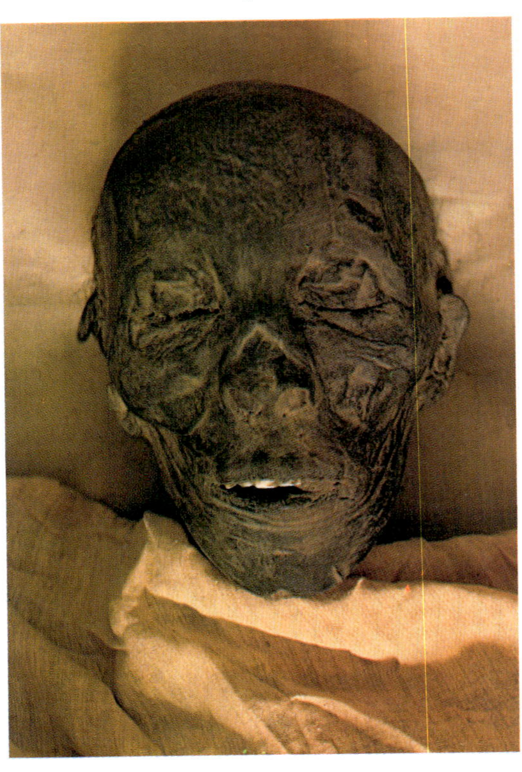

covers a substance spread over all the body. This substance is vulgarly called *gras de cadavre*; it covers the bones.' It is fair to conclude that the presence of adipocere is easily recognised and verified by a medical examiner, and without doubt would have been noted in any post-mortem examinations of the allegedly incorrupt since dissection could hardly have failed to reveal it.

True incorruption triumphs over the condition of the body, the circumstances of the burial and the normal processes of decomposition. For some reason a certain body stays intact while others, in the same place, rot into

Left: an ancient Egyptian mummy, thousands of years old, now on show at Cairo Museum. This man was the beneficiary of the embalmers' highly-developed skills, though they were not bought cheaply. Ironically, the last resting places of the poor – not elaborate tombs, but just the hot sands of the desert – have proved to be the best preserving agent

In death as in life

The official opening of William the Conqueror's tomb at the Church of St Etienne, or L'Abbaye-aux-hommes, in Caen, north-west France, in 1552 caused great amazement. For although the soldier-king had been entombed for over 400 years his body – and particularly his face – remained remarkably well-preserved and lifelike. It is true that he had been embalmed, but in the rather primitive fashion of his day; a body treated in this way would normally have turned to dust many years before.

A local artist was commissioned to paint William's posthumous portrait (left); he used the corpse as a model, but chose to dress him in contemporary clothes. Thus William the Conqueror became the image of an early Renaissance prince.

the dust from whence they came. The Catholic Church sees it as a 'divine favour' to a pious soul, although it is not, on its own, enough for beatification (except in the Russian Orthodox Church). Joan Cruz summarises the value of the relics for Catholics: 'For those of us who have loved and admired certain of these saints, it is a comfort of sorts to know that they are not just somewhere in the great realms beyond, but that their actual bodies, which will one day be made glorious, are still present among us.'

But objective researchers are not blessed with such certainty, for they see authenticated cases occurring outside the Catholic Church, and in most cultures. Nor is incorruption restricted to the saintly. A secular case, typical of the form in which one might encounter it in folklore, was reported in the *News of the World* on 8 May 1977. It concerned Nadja Mattei, who died in Rome in 1965, aged two. Her mother claimed that for 12 years her dead daughter came to her in dreams begging to be fetched from her coffin. Early in 1977 the authorities granted her request for exhumation, and baby Nadja's body was found to be quite free of putrefaction.

Authenticated true incorruption is very rare, and each story, both in the religious context and outside it, has a similar structure: an incorrupt body, an eerie persistent fragrance, and frequently some attendant paranormal phenomena, such as strange lights around the grave or revelation of incorruption through a dream. The universal similarity in these accounts suggests some kind of archetypal event that transcends ordinary reality. The questions it raises strike to the core of the nature of our physical and spiritual existence, and the nature of reality itself.

Is this the face of Christ?

Was the image on the famous Turin shroud made by the body of Christ himself – or is it no more than a painting by a medieval forger? FRANK SMYTH charts the remarkable history of this most controversial of relics

Left: St Veronica's cloth, in a detail from a 16th-century window in St John's Church, Gouda, Holland. Legend has it that, as Christ carried the cross to Golgotha, St Veronica was so moved by pity that she gave him her handkerchief to wipe his face. Later she found that the image of his face had been miraculously impressed upon it. A relic preserved in St Peter's, Rome, was long thought to be St Veronica's cloth, but this claim is no longer taken seriously

Right: the Turin shroud. The impressions of the front and back of a man's body can be clearly seen, 'hinged' at the head

DURING AND IMMEDIATELY after the Crusades, mendicant friars wandered Europe selling objects said to have come from the Holy Land – allegedly relics of the early church. Among those recorded were the knucklebones of St Peter, the arrows that killed St Sebastian, pieces of the Virgin's gown and lumps of dried bread from the Last Supper. The very ubiquity of some of these items made the Church a laughing stock and gave ammunition to such reformers as Martin Luther and John Calvin; there are still said, for instance, to be enough splinters of the true cross scattered among the churches of Italy, Spain, and southern France to make a sizeable grove of trees.

Not unnaturally the Roman Catholic Church became wary of, if not openly hostile towards, such artefacts, and at the end of the 19th century the Vatican issued a proclamation stating that no relic, 'be it the most sacred in Christendom', could be regarded as authentic. This bald edict was made to counter the remarkable assertion of a French scientist and agnostic that a strip of cloth known as the Holy Shroud of Turin was the genuine winding sheet of Christ. Such was

Above: Pope Clement VII, who reigned from 1523 to 1534. The Bishop of Troyes complained to him that the Turin shroud was being exhibited for financial gain by its owner, Sir Geoffrey de Charnay. The Pope, however, ruled that the shroud could stay on show, but not as an authentic relic

the standing of this Dr Yves Delage, however, that science took over where superstition left off; for the past 80 years continued attempts have been made to unravel the mystery of the shroud, culminating in the Shroud of Turin Research Project of October 1978. For five days the fabric was subjected to exhaustive tests by nearly 40 top scientists using space-age instruments, but when the full analysis of their work was published, it became clear that the project posed as many questions as it answered.

The Holy Shroud of Turin is a rectangular strip of cloth 13½ feet (4 metres) long by three and a half feet (1 metre) wide. On its surface can be seen the faint, yellowish-brown imprint of a human figure, naked and bearded. Darker stains, said to be blood, are superimposed on the image, notably on the head, wrists, feet, and left hand side, and both back and front views of the figure appear, hinged, as it were, at the crown of the head, which appears to bear a kind of wreath.

The first probable mention of the shroud occurs in 1203, when the military chronicler Robert de Clari wrote that in the previous year he had seen a *sydoine* – shroud – that bore 'the figure of our Lord' during the sacking of Constantinople by Christian knights during the Fourth Crusade. Unfortunately, he said, it had disappeared in the turmoil. Just over 150 years later comes the first certain record of the present 'Turin' shroud, and all the indications are that it was the same as that seen by de Clari. It was owned by a rather unscrupulous knight

Left: a painting of Christ on the cross by the 19th-century French artist Delacroix. Like other traditional artistic representations, it shows Christ nailed to the cross through the feet and the palms of the hands. Research has shown, however, that the flesh of the palms of the hands cannot support the weight of the body without tearing. It is highly likely that, as in the Turin shroud image, the nails were driven through the radius of the wrist. The authentic detail of the position of the nails in the shroud image supports the argument that it is not a medieval forgery

Below: ex-King Umberto of Italy, Duke of Savoy and owner of the Turin shroud, who died in 1983. Although the shroud had been in the possession of the Dukes of Savoy since 1578, he bequeathed it to the Vatican

named Geoffrey de Charney, overlord of the French town of Lirey, and by 1389 the fame of the relic was such that he decided to put it on public display for money. This move caused a great deal of jealousy in neighbourhood circles, for popular relics were at a premium at that time and the financial income from a good one could be considerable. Either out of pure jealousy or perhaps because he thought he was acting from honourable motives, the Bishop of Troyes complained to Pope Clement VII at Avignon of de Charney's exposition. His story was the foundation of the most frequent accusation levelled at the shroud until the present day: that it was in fact a forgery, the work of an artist . . . 'cunningly painted, the truth being attested by the artist who painted it'.

Pope Clement seems to have thought the Bishop's allegation a trifle thin, and ruled that the shroud could remain on show as an object of devotion, though not necessarily as an 'authentic' relic.

Saved from the fire

For over 60 years the shroud continued to attract pilgrims, until in 1453 Geoffrey's grand-daughter Marguerite de Charney gave it – or more likely sold it, though the motive is not clear – to Louis, Duke of Savoy. The de Charneys had shown the relic in a simple setting, but Louis, either from piety or showmanship, encased it in a silver frame and built a special shrine – Sainte Chapelle – at Chambéry, his capital. In 1532 a near-disastrous fire broke out in Sainte Chapelle; the heat melted the silver reliquary, and drops of molten metal burned through the cloth in several places, though water was quickly used to douse the scorching. The worst burns were neatly patched, and both the burns and the water stains were to be of assistance during the 1978 scientific investigation. In 1578 the shroud made its last journey across the Alps to Piedmont, where the then Duke of Savoy had set up his household at Turin. It was lodged in the cathedral and has remained there, apart from a spell during the last war, ever since. Until his death in 1983, it was the property of ex-King Umberto (also Duke of Savoy) who was exiled in Portugal. He left it to the Vatican, but it is still kept in Turin Cathedral, looked after by 'his' Archbishop, Anastasio Ballestreno.

From the very beginning of its recorded history, observers had noted something subtly but indefinably 'wrong' about the image on the shroud. Pope Clement, for instance, is said to have felt that if it was a forgery, far from being 'cunningly painted' as the Bishop of Troyes alleged, it was rather badly done. Albrecht Dürer examined it at Ste Chapelle in the early part of the 16th century and was baffled by it. He made several attempts to draw it, but felt that, though the anatomical proportions were correct, the model for it must have been

Above: a photographic negative of the face from the Turin shroud. There are clear marks around the forehead – made, perhaps, by the crown of thorns?

'deformed' – in a manner he found hard to define.

It was not until 1898 that the shroud revealed its first strange secret. It was taken from its silver casket to be put on rare public display, and a Turin photographer, Secondo Pia, was commissioned to take the first photographs of it. As he developed his plates there appeared not the blurred, odd image on the shroud but the perfectly formed features of a man: the shroud itself was a photographic negative. The realisation so astounded Pia, he said, that he dropped the plate he was holding in shock.

The implications of the discovery were not lost on Dr Yves Delage, a prominent physicist and zoologist and leading member of the French Academy of Sciences. He determined to find out how the image had appeared – 500 years before the invention of photography. However, his motives were not disinterested, for Dr Delage was an agnostic and militantly anti-Catholic, and he had no intention of allowing the Church to make supernatural claims for the shroud.

For three years he and a brilliant young biologist named Paul Joseph Vignon studied the image and experimented with methods of reproducing it. First, they employed artists to paint an image using medieval pigments, pursuing the theory that the painting might have faded in such a way that the darker areas had become highlights over the years, thus producing a 'negative' image. None of the experiments was successful.

Then they began again from the premise that the cloth had been *somebody's* shroud. The cloth was of Palestinian weave of a type known to have been made until the fifth century AD. Execution by crucifixion had been outlawed by the Romans in the fourth century, so the man of the shroud had been crucified in Palestine some time before then. They noted that, according to biblical traditions, Christ had been hastily buried on Friday to avoid the Jewish sabbath. The body had been 'anointed' but not washed. The most common form of burial ointments in use in Palestine at that time had been myrrh and aloes. Vignon knew that sweat from a dead body produces a substance named urea, which in decay gives off ammonia vapour. He experimented with ammonia and cloth 'sensitised' with myrrh and aloes, and managed to produce brownish stains similar to those on the shroud.

As far as Delage was concerned, that was the answer to the riddle of the image's formation. But when he presented his findings to the Academy of Sciences in 1902, he went further. He was convinced, he said, that this was indeed Christ's shroud. On the one hand, he pointed out, there was the biblical account of a man who had undergone a very uncharacteristic form of crucifixion; as well as being nailed to a cross he had also been scourged, crowned with thorns, and finally pierced through the left side with a lance. On the other hand, here was a strip of linen apparently originating in Palestine depicting a man who had undergone exactly the same form of torture and death. Delage added that his conclusion did not affect his own anti-religious views in any way. He regarded the shroud as a piece of historical evidence, and pointed out that if such weighty evidence had involved a relic of some character from mythology such as Achilles it would be accepted much more easily. As it was, the emotional aura surrounding his conclusion served only to obscure scientific reality.

There is no doubt that Delage was right on this point. The predominantly Roman Catholic Academy were nervous of the implications, and rejected his findings – even taking the rare step of suppressing them by refusing to print his carefully mustered evidence in their minutes.

Analysing the Turin shroud

The ghostly image on the Turin shroud has been an enigma for centuries. Recent research has revealed some of its startling secrets, but the mystery seems as deep as ever

AFTER THE FRENCH ACADEMY OF SCIENCES rejected the findings of Dr Yves Delage – that the Turin shroud was indeed the shroud of Christ – the subject remained in abeyance for 30 years. Then, in 1932, another Frenchman, a forensic pathologist named Dr Pierre Barbet, began to look at the image from a medical point of view, taking advantage of a much clearer set of photographs taken the previous year.

The first point to intrigue Dr Barbet was the position of the nail wounds in the wrists, rather than through the palms as tradition-ally depicted. Experimenting with cadavers he discovered that the flesh of the hands will not support the weight of a dead body, let alone a living, writhing one – the flesh very quickly tears away. As crucifixion had not taken place since the fourth century AD traditional painters were not to know this: why then, would a medieval forger have such specialised knowledge? Barbet discovered that the only secure way to crucify a body would be to place the nails through the radius of the wrist, as in the shroud. Furthermore a nail placed in this way would damage the median nerve, causing the thumbs to retract involuntarily into the palms of the hand – again a little-known piece of evidence that was embodied in the shroud figure. The 'blood' stains around the shroud figure's side wound also showed the marks of a clear liquid – tallying with the biblical description of 'blood and water' issuing from Christ's side. Now death from crucifixion comes, not from loss of blood, but from asphyxia and shock. The lungs are compressed by the stretched position of the body; the victim hauls himself up by the nails securing his feet and wrists, thus allowing himself to take a

breath but causing intense agony. Every movement progressively weakens the victim, so that eventually he can no longer pull himself up and suffocates. Suffocation causes mucus to collect in the base of the lungs, and Barbet was able to show that a lance thrust in the side would pierce the tip of the left lung, releasing this liquid.

Dr Barbet's crisp and clinical report did a great deal to revive the interest of orthodox scientists in the nature of the shroud, and international 'sindonologists' – they took their name from the Greek for shroud – began to press for a full scientific exami-nation. It was not until the 1970s, however, that ex-King Umberto gradually yielded to the pressure. To put an accurate date on the cloth itself was one of the priorities, but the obvious modern way of doing this – by using the Carbon 14 process – would involve destroying a portion of the shroud, and Umberto was reluctant on this point. Instead, in 1973, two top European scientists were invited to use more orthodox methods. Professor Max Frei, a leading Swiss forensic scientist, and Professor Gilbert Raes, an expert on fabrics from the University of Ghent in Belgium, were given access to the cloth. First, the pair reported that 'the image was completely superficial, in that the top-most fibrils [minute strands] of the threads only were affected. No pigmentation could be seen even under magnification.'

Frei took dust particles for laboratory analysis, and found 48 different samples of pollen. The identification of pollen grains, which survive almost indefinitely even in the most unlikely conditions, is one of the most precise processes of modern forensic science. Most of the seeds were from France and

Above: Dr Ray Rogers, Dr John Jackson and Professor Giovanni Riggi, of the Shroud of Turin Research Project, take their first look at the underside of the shroud in October 1978. For five days, the researchers subjected the shroud to a series of 'non-destructive' tests using ultra-modern equipment. Full details of their findings have still to be published, but the scientists seem to have raised as many questions as they have answered

Northern Italy, as expected, but seven proved to be from halophylic (or salt-loving) plants usually found around the Dead Sea and certain other parts of Palestine. Though interesting circumstantially, this was not definite evidence of the shroud's origin, as pollen travels great distances on the wind and may have been transmitted on the clothing of travellers – the image had been openly exhibited during its early recorded history,

Gilbert Raes had removed small samples of threads, however, and his evidence proved to be supportive. Middle-Eastern cotton plants had been used to make the linen, which was of a herringbone twill weave, quite expensive compared with the normal plain weave of Palestine, and the thread had been hand-spun, although all European thread was spun by wheel after about AD 1150. The threads had also been bleached before weaving – an extremely archaic practice.

In 1974, came a breakthrough as important in its way as the discovery that the shroud was a photographic negative. Two US Air Force scientists, John Jackson and Eric Jumper, scanned pictures of the shroud with a complex instrument called the VP-8 Image

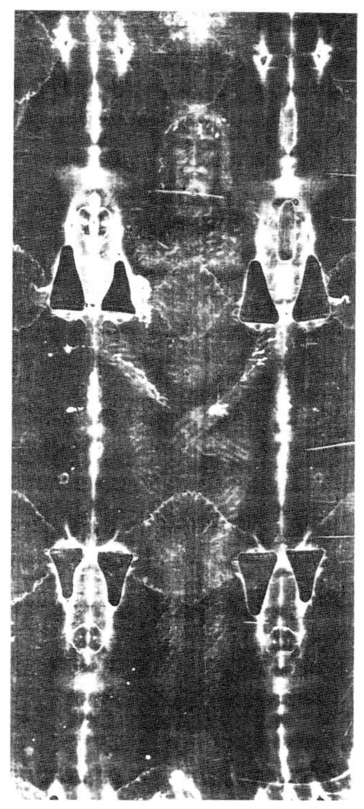

Above: the shroud as it appears on a photographic negati·e. The distinctive paralle lines of scars that cover he surface of the body are of a type that could have been made by Roman *flagrae* – two-thonged whips tipped with lead or bone

Left and right: two views of a three-dimensional model of the head on the shroud made in 1963 by Leo Vala, an experimental photographer. Leo Vala produced his model by projecting a photographic negative of the face onto clay and shaping the features according to the depth of shadow projected

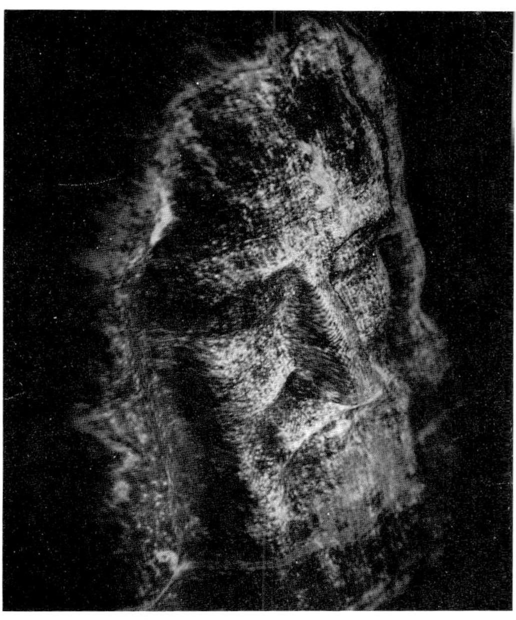

Analyser. Using a computer in conjunction with the VP-8 they were able to build a three-dimensional model of the man of the shroud in laminated cardboard. It was this development that finally convinced a group of US scientists that the shroud was worthy of intensive study, and in March 1977 the Shroud of Turin Research Project was given permission by ex-King Umberto to go ahead with 'non-destructive' tests.

On 8 October 1978, after a public exposition, the shroud was removed from its nitrogen-filled container and taken to the Turin royal palace where it was scrutinised by 36 scientists who had brought with them 72 cases of ultra-modern equipment. They included physicists, biochemists, forensic

scientists, pathologists, microphotography specialists, analysts and – somewhat incongruously – leading representatives from the US Nuclear Technology Corporation.

The report of the teams' findings has now been published in full but, despite one major clash of opinion, the mystery of the shroud seems as deep as ever. The one major dissenter among the 36 principal scientists involved was Dr Walter C. McCrone, head of a private firm of chemical analysts based in Chicago. It was Dr McCrone who proved that the ink on the so-called 'Viking' Vinland Map was of medieval origin, and his opinion on the shroud followed similar lines – although he admitted that he was not present at the main session at the royal palace and apparently worked from samples.

In a series of lectures in Britain in September 1980, he said that his microscopic tests revealed stains from iron oxide, a constituent of traditional artist's materials. 'Though how the artist did it I cannot say,' he said. 'I believe the shroud is a fake but I cannot prove it.' He thought a carbon date test would give the date as 14th century: 'it was very fashionable to make frauds at that time. I understand that the rest of the group are not going to say whether the shroud is authentic or not. They will probably say that the image comes closest to being similar to, and that they cannot distinguish it from, a burn image. Where they go from there I don't know.'

One of the principal chemical investigators, Ray Rogers of the Los Alamos National Scientific Laboratory, found that the image consisted of a light yellowish colouring that appeared only on the very top surface of the fibrils. The colouring was not 'diffused, soaked into, run down the sides of or deposited between threads' as it would have been if pigment had been painted on or rubbed in. Here the fire of 1532 had been helpful; heat sufficient to burn the cloth

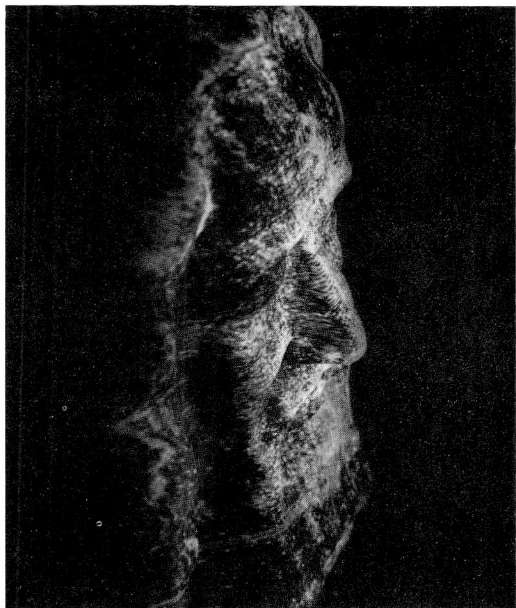

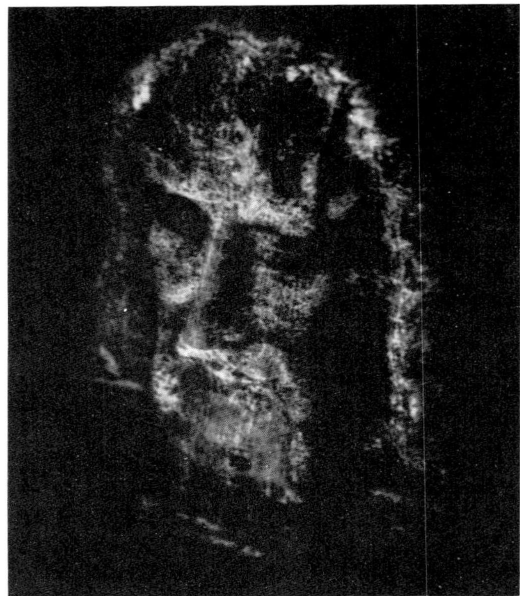

should have altered the surrounding colouring of any pigment, but it had not done so. There was a total evenness right up to the edge of the scorch holes. Furthermore the water used to douse the flames would have caused water-colour or ink marks to run, but had not done so. In 1980, Rogers said:

Most of us are now convinced that the shroud is not a painting. Except for a small amount of iron oxide we found no pigment whatsoever. And we do not think that either liquid or vapour could have produced the image we see.

Spectroscopist Sam Pellicori of Santa Barbara Research Center had set out to examine the 'vaporographic' theory of Delage and Vignon – that the image had been caused by a chemical reaction from body sweat and spices. But, he explained, the image shows traces on the face and other places where the cloth would not have touched:

The process of the formation of the image on the shroud is baffling. I can best describe it as a boiling up of the surface material of the outer threads. Certain evidence indicates that this may have been caused by a violent burst of radiant heat.

The 'bloodstains' on the image came in, of course, for extensive scrutiny. The first, and most important point, was that they had been deposited in the normal way; they showed up as 'positive' in the 'negative' shroud, and when the backing cloth, sewn to the linen in the 16th century, was lifted, it was found that they had soaked right through – unlike the image itself. Dr John Heller of the New England Institute said that none of the tests had shown that the ancient stains were not blood, but several had indicated that they could be. The stains were ringed with microscopic secondary stains that were remarkably like those left by serum – a clear liquid squeezed out by blood clotting. Ultraviolet tests had caused the bloodstains to

Left and right: two more views of Leo Vala's clay model of the man of the Turin shroud. It was a similar three-dimensional model, built in 1974 by two Americans, that convinced scientists that the shroud warranted intensive study

fluoresce, and x-rays had revealed the exact percentage of iron for positive blood tests. Most importantly, Dr Heller found tiny crystals between the threads on the bloodstained areas that he considered to be haemoglobin 'altered by age'.

The shape and direction of the stains themselves were 'authentic', as if a newly crucified body had been involved. Stains from the wrist wounds, for instance, ran up the forearms to the elbows – exactly as would occur with the arms in a crucified position. Furthermore, blood from the wound in the side had run down and collected under the small of the back – another authentic detail. Finally, the entire surface of the body from neck to ankles was covered in scars in parallel pairs – apparently the marks of scourging. These formed the pattern that would be made by two torturers wielding Roman *flagrae* – two-thonged whips with pieces of lead or bone at the tips – a form of scourging that

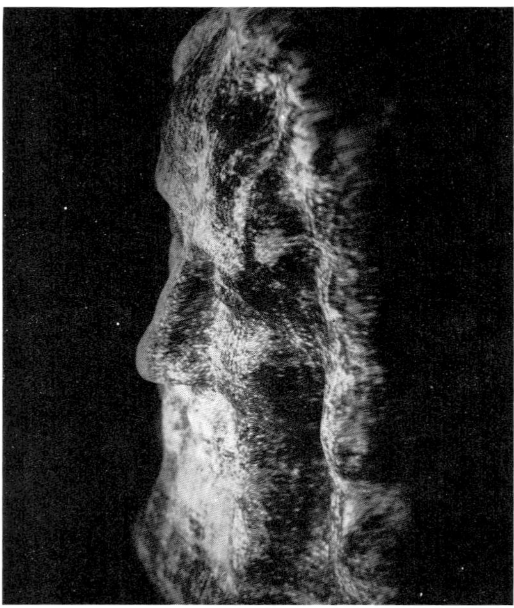

fitted with known Roman practice.

It seems to have been decided that the carbon dating process cannot give a result exact enough to justify the destruction of a small part of the shroud that would be entailed, given that a study of the cloth has already established that it dates from before the fourth century.

There remain two great question marks over the holy shroud of Turin. First: if the image was produced by a 'burst of radiant heat' what caused it?

And second, the question asked in 1902 by Yves Delage of the French Academy of Sciences: 'If it is not Christ's shroud, then whose is it? Surely not that of some common malefactor?'

As Kenneth Weaver, science editor of the *National Geographic* magazine and observer at the test session, commented: 'That, say both scientists and theologians, will remain forever outside the bounds of proof.'

The Old Testament is full of 'signs and wonders', miraculous events that seem frankly impossible to the sceptic. But, as DAVID CHRISTIE-MURRAY shows, they bear a similarity to many paranormal events down the ages

THE BIBLE CONSISTS OF 66 books (80 including the Apocrypha) written over about a millennium, although some of its material is derived from far older oral tradition. Like most ancient writings it recounts paranormal incidents, though a student of psychical research will be surprised by their comparative absence and the general soberness of the history. Psychical researchers have, however, investigated the Bible comparatively little, partly because of a distrust of records so ancient by writers with such different outlooks from their own, partly because they hold that it is psychical research that throws light upon the Bible, not the Bible that contributes to psychical research.

Many people also feel that Holy Writ is sacrosanct, the Word of God, to be accepted, not studied – except as a guide to devotion and righteous living – and never to be criticised. Others see in it no more value than is contained in any collection of ancient writings. But it is possible to take a middle way: one can apply the principles of scholarly criticism to the Bible as to any other book, though without preconceptions, recognising that further discoveries are continually modifying present knowledge, and respecting the views of others. Whatever the findings of modern critics, the book has a unique value, recording the evolution of the conception of God from primitive animism to the most ethical monotheism, influencing three major religions, Islam, Judaism and Christianity.

Certain types of paranormal activity are

For it is written...

Above: Jacob's momentous dream of the ladder that reached down from heaven, upon which angels climb. The Lord spoke to him, bestowing on him the land on which he slept, adding: 'For I will not leave thee . . .'. Could this dream have been a subconscious safety mechanism to reassure the exiled Jacob and to give him a sense of purpose? Whatever its cause, it drastically altered not only his own life, but that of the entire Israelite nation

Right: Saul consults the 'witch' of Endor, who was probably a medium. Such consultations were strictly forbidden by Judaic law

missing in the Old Testament because its editors were followers of Yahweh (Jehovah), whose worship included prohibitions such as, 'Thou shalt not suffer a witch to live.' Their 'good' kings annihilated those with familiar spirits (mediums). Only one account of spiritist activity in Israel is extant, that of Saul's visit to the medium – 'the witch' – at Endor, to enquire his fate of the dead prophet, Samuel (1 Samuel 28). That visit is recorded as his final sin against God.

Other paranormal phenomena in the Old Testament include divination, possibly dowsing, precognitive dreams, mystical experiences, healing and precognition.

Divination had to be carried out under the auspices of Yahweh. Old Testament 'prophets' were regarded not as diviners but as religious and political commentators, and therefore were judged to be 'true' or 'false' not so much by the accuracy of their forecasts as by the gods they followed. The prophets of Baal were 'false' because their god was Yahweh's rival, whereas Jeremiah was 'true', even though his oracles were sometimes

Right: Elijah is taken up by God in a 'chariot of fire' and disappears from the sight of men. Some modern writers believe that this is a primitive description of a UFO abduction, while many consider the language visionary, as in Blake's *Jerusalem*: 'Bring me my bow of burning gold, bring me my chariot of fire . . . . But whatever really happened, the Bible records several sudden disappearances, mainly of the chosen prophets of the Lord

Far right: Moses hears the Lord speaking to him from the burning bush. Was this an hallucination – or genuine paranormal combustion?

Above: Joseph finds favour with Pharaoh by interpreting his dreams. The dream of seven healthy cattle being eaten by seven lean cattle Joseph interpreted as a prediction of seven years of prosperity being followed by seven years of famine. This happened, but because of the dream's warning Pharaoh had been able to build up stocks of food for the time of famine. Modern psychologists have confirmed that we often dream in symbols – such as cattle – and precognitive dreams may be widespread, but unfortunately such dreams are often ignored

mistaken, because he served Jehovah. So Yahweh's high priest was provided with means of divination, 'the Urim and the Thummim' ('Lights and Truths'), apparently semi-precious stones set in his breastplate, which he may have used for a kind of crystal-gazing (Exodus 28). But on the whole, individuals devised their own methods of divination or of reading meaning into symbolical 'signs'. Thus Gideon knew that God would grant him victory because one night dew fell on a fleece while the ground around was dry and the next night the process was reversed (Judges 6).

Moses, finding water in the desert by the use of his rod (Exodus 17 and Numbers 20), may have used dowsing techniques. But though a visionary, he was no dreamer, and revelatory dreams are possibly the commonest paranormal phenomena in the Old Testament. Jacob's ladder dream (Genesis 28) repeated the promise made to his grandfather, Abraham, that his descendants should possess the very land on which the vision was dreamed. Joseph dreamed of his future lordship over his family (Genesis 37) and foresaw from the dreams of Pharaoh's imprisoned butler and baker that the former would be restored and the latter executed. His successful interpretation of Pharaoh's dreams foretelling seven years of plenty followed by seven of famine – of seven healthy kine (cattle) being eaten by seven feeble kine – resulted in his own promotion to high office (Genesis 40).

Dreams of yesterday

In the light of modern dream research, from experiments carried out by such agencies as the Maimonides Dream Laboratory, we could conclude that these dreams happened as recorded. Jacob, leaving territory in which he had spent his youth, with thoughts that it might be for ever, could have been comforted by his dreams reminding him of God's promise to Abraham, which in turn made his own return probable. Joseph, knowing the reasons for the butler's and baker's imprisonment, needed no remarkable insight to interpret correctly the symbolism of their hope and fear.

The mystical experiences of different individuals vary in type and intensity. At a crisis of his life, Jacob wrestles with a mysterious but beneficial supernatural being (Genesis 32). An angel (that is, a messenger – not necessarily supernatural, though often so) appears to Samson's parents, foretelling their hero son's birth, and leaves them by ascending in an altar flame (Judges 13). The child Samuel, first of the great biblical prophets, has his first experience as a sensitive when he clairaudiently hears the voice of

God (1 Samuel 3). Every prophet seems to have had similar experiences, from Isaiah's vision in the Temple of 'the Lord . . . high and lifted up', attended by seraphim (Isaiah 6), to Ezekiel's sight of four great rings, full of eyes, their motion accompanied by a rushing sound (Ezekiel 1).

Other questions arise when one considers the wonder-stories surrounding the biblical folk heroes. Around individuals such as King Arthur and Robin Hood, who have a kernel of historicity, tales gather that are self-evidently legendary accretions. While fundamentalists deny that the Bible contains anything of the kind, most scholars would say that many stories, such as those of Samson's carrying away the city gates of Gaza (Judges 16) and Elisha making iron float (2 Kings 6), are of this kind, and that every account must be examined according to the principles of normal historical and literary criticism. A balance must be held.

Modern knowledge shows that some incidents that would have been considered pure legend at the beginning of the 20th century are at least possible, especially in the realm of healing. Although healing comes into its own in the New Testament, there are a few examples of paranormal healing in the Old Testament. Miriam, punished with leprosy for a revolt against Moses, is restored by his prayer (Numbers 12). Gazing upon the brazen image of a serpent heals Israelites bitten by snakes in the wilderness (Numbers 21). The image survived until its superstitious veneration caused it to be destroyed by Hezekiah, King of Judah, himself cured of an otherwise fatal abscess by a fig poultice. This event was signalled by a marked retreat of the shadow on the sundial (2 Kings 20), an event for which fundamentalist apologists claim there is astronomical evidence. Naaman, the Syrian general, was cured of leprosy by distant healing when Elisha, without seeing him, sent a message instructing him to bathe in the river Jordan seven times (2 Kings 5). Elijah restored a dead boy to life by stretching himself three times upon him (1 Kings 17). Elisha apparently used a 'kiss-of-life' technique on another, placing 'his mouth upon his mouth, and his eyes upon his eyes, and his hands upon his hands; and he stretched himself upon the child: and the flesh of the child waxed warm' (2 Kings 4). Since there are, in the literature of psychotherapy and psychical research, well-attested instances of chronic skin diseases being cured by hypnosis, and others of cures being effected by mental action at a distance, it would be unwise to reject dogmatically the possible truth of these stories.

And there are several other parallels with unexplained phenomena today. Mysterious disappearances were seen to occur then as now. Genesis 5:24 states dramatically that 'Enoch walked with God: and he was not: for God took him.' Moses was cryptically recorded as being 'buried by God' (Deuteronomy 34) – where is not known – but Josephus, the Jewish historian, records a tradition that 'a cloud stood over him [Moses] of a sudden and he disappeared in a certain valley.' And Elisha tells of Elijah's departure alive in 'the fiery chariot' (2 Kings 2).

Paranormal fire occurs frequently in the Old Testament, not unparalleled today if the collection of stories about spontaneous human combustion are true. Such could have been the poetic justice of the rebels Nadab and Abihu, devoured by fire for offering 'strange fire' before the Lord in rivalry to Aaron, the appointed high priest (Numbers 3). The spontaneous combustion of 250 other rebels (Numbers 16) is more difficult to accept, though one can imagine the possible occurrence and exaggerated report of a number of deaths occurring simultaneously from

Right: God shows his power by igniting his prophet Elijah's sacrifice – while that of the Baal worshippers remains unlit, despite their frantic pleas. Spontaneous combustion is common in the Bible – and, according to Charles Fort and other collectors of tales of anomalous phenomena, not unknown in the lives of ordinary people even today

Below: the 'pillar of cloud' that assured the Israelites of God's presence during the daytime

The literal truth?

A river that turns to blood, plagues of frogs, and the mysterious deaths of the firstborn – these are among the plagues of Egypt as recorded in the Old Testament. Even many theologians maintain that these afflictions cannot possibly have happened as described, although similar events are recorded today.

Red rain fell in Newfoundland in 1890; frogs cascaded onto a bewildered Athens in 1980, and the large hailstones that fell near Clermond-Ferrand, France, in 1873 did no harm for they fell *slowly*. And on 14 June 1880 red, blue and grey hailstones fell in rapid succession in one small area of Russia.

Grievous afflictions such as the deaths of the Egyptian firstborn could well have been the effects of a curse for, as reports suggest, curses can work, and often do. The plagues, and other paranormal manifestations such as the parting of the Red Sea (left), may have been brought about by Moses himself, using psychic means. American parapsychologist Rex G. Stanford's revolutionary theory of psi-mediated instrumental response – PMIR – suggests that otherwise ordinary people can psychically cause things to go their way, but only when in extreme need. But Moses was no ordinary man and his people were being threatened with extinction – a combination that may well have unleashed formidable powers.

lightning. Cloud and fire were symbols of the divine presence, cherubim and seraphim being originally cloud and lightning spirits. The Israelites were led through the wilderness by a 'pillar of cloud' by day and a 'pillar of fire' by night (Exodus 13), though for those who like rational explanations, the smoke and fire may have come from a brazier carried at the head of the wanderers – for them, however, it may have been none the less symbolic of God's guidance.

On many occasions God 'answers by fire' in mysterious ways, though the origins of the stories may often lie in priestly legerdemain. Heaven-sent fire ignites altars for Moses and Aaron (Leviticus 9), Gideon (Judges 6), David (1 Chronicles 21) and Solomon (2 Chronicles 7). Elijah calls down divine fire to consume bands of men sent to apprehend him (2 Kings 1). The supreme example of God's fire is in the dramatic scene on Mount Carmel, when Elijah's sacrifice, drenched with water, bursts into flame after Baal's prophets had failed to win fire from their god to ignite their offering (1 Kings 18). Perhaps, say the rationalists, lightning, preceding the storm that ended three years of drought, ignited Elijah's sacrifice. Or does the answer lie in conjuring tricks, or the fictional accretions of folk legend? Are all such 'paranormal' events explicable by natural law? After so many centuries, nothing can be proved or disproved.

Other instances of apparent paranormalities in the Bible could well have had natural causes. The 'burning bush' from which God's voice called Moses to lead Israel from Egypt (Exodus 3) could have been a wisp of

Joshua and his men, having marched repeatedly around the walls of Jericho, sound their trumpets – and the walls crumble. Some modern commentators suggest that the vibrations set up by the marching were reinforced by the bugle blast, having a disastrous effect on walls that were perhaps already in a state of bad repair

gas escaping from the oil-rich desert and ignited by the Sun's rays, concentrated by the burning glass of a crystalline stone. Flickering in the wind, it could have looked like a bush blowing from side to side. The plagues of Egypt (Exodus 7) could have occurred because excessive deposits of red clay turned the water to stagnant 'blood', which bred an excess of frogs whose piled-up, decaying bodies bred 'lice', the larvae of swarms of flies that caused the horrifying disease in cattle and the 'plague of boils' in humans. The crossing of the 'Red' – or 'Reed' – Sea can be explained in different

ways according to the various locations where the crossing may have occurred. It has been suggested that the similar miracle, which occurred years later, of the dry-shod crossing of the river Jordan (Joshua 4) was caused by the temporary blocking of the river by an earth tremor. The same tremor could so have weakened Jericho's walls (shown archaeologically to have been shoddily built) that the rhythmic tramping round them of the Israelite army and the resonance of the blast of the rams' horns were enough to 'bring them tumbling down' (Joshua 6).

Bread of heaven?

Crossing the desert the Israelites were fed with 'manna' from heaven. This is widely believed to have been the exudation of tamarisk shrubs, which is still used as food by Bedouin. It is, however, produced only in small quantities, and the paranormality of the biblical account lies in the quantity produced – enough to feed an entire nation – and the fact that twice as much was produced every Friday so that the work of gathering manna should not profane the Saturday Sabbath. And Elijah was fed morning and evening by 'ravens', which brought him meat and bread. But the Hebrew word for ravens is the same as that for 'merchants' or 'Arabs'.

Nearly a quarter of the Old Testament is occupied by writings of the political commentators known as the 'prophets'. Precognition – 'prophesying' – is therefore the paranormal phenomenon most associated with it, for in popular thought prophets foretell the future. There are indeed many stories of prophecies that were fulfilled, most of which can be paralleled in other cultures. One example is Elisha's forecast that within a day the starving city of Samaria, besieged by the Syrians, would have a wealth of provisions, and that a certain lord, who had scorned his prophecy, should see the food

The Israelites gather manna in the desert. Rationalists say that the sticky, sweetish substance must have been the exudation of the tamarisk shrub. However, the manna appeared in precisely the right amount, even according to individual appetite, and twice as much appeared on Fridays to avoid breaking the law by collecting it on the Saturday Sabbath. It seems possible that some paranormal mechanism was involved, but whether induced by some outside intelligence – 'the Lord' – or through the psychokinetic powers of Moses we shall never know

but not eat it. Against all expectations the food arrived; the lord, supervising its distribution at the city gates, was trampled to death in the rush for it (2 Kings 7).

When the prophets spoke of the future they nearly always did so conditionally – if you do not walk in God's way, this [disaster] will happen; if you do, it will not. Other prophecies are not what they seem. 'Behold a virgin shall conceive and bear a son' (Isaiah 7:14) is not, as widely believed, a prophecy of the virgin birth of Christ. The word that was translated as 'virgin' means, in fact, a young married woman. The text continues: 'For before the child shall know to refuse the evil, and choose the good, the land that thou abhorrest shall be forsaken of both her kings.' It seems that Isaiah in effect pointed at a pregnant young woman – possibly his own wife – and indicated that King Ahaz's two enemies would be destroyed before the child could grow up. This is one case where a parochial interpretation of the text makes most sense.

The prophets aimed not so much at foretelling the future as at describing what they saw as the will of God in the circumstances of their time. But in doing this, their prophecies *were* fulfilled, often in ways more profound and long-lasting than they ever imagined. Isaiah's 'virgin' statement is one example of this. These multi-meaning prophecies that reverberated down the ages culminated, Christian scholars claim, in the miraculous life of Jesus Christ in the New Testament.

Jonah emerges from his ordeal in the stomach of a whale. As with the Old Testament book of Daniel, there is no point in assuming a literal interpretation, for both books were written as fictional moral tracts

His wonders to perform

Levitation, psychokinesis, ESP and paranormal healing are all, apparently, described in the New Testament. But did the conventions of the gospel writers obscure the facts? Were they as miraculous as reported?

IF JESUS WAS GOD incarnate, as Christianity teaches, his life could scarcely be expected to be anything but miraculous. Beginning with a virgin birth (a claim not made for him until after his death), an event surrounded with portents – as was the birth of his cousin, John the Baptist – the Bible implies that he lived an uneventful life until he was about 30. Then he burst on his world like a meteor. For some three to four years he taught and worked miracles in Palestine and, if the records can be believed, whatever else he was, he was the greatest and most beneficent healer who has ever lived. By his followers he came to be recognised as the all-conquering Messiah whose coming had been foretold by the prophets. They could not, however, accept his teaching that his kingdom was spiritual, not political, and they were appalled when he went unresisting to execution. To the members of the Jewish religious establishment whose authority he challenged he was a dangerous upstart who might cause trouble with their political masters, the Romans. According to the gospels, the climax came at the Passover festival, when the chief priests allied with an unwilling Roman governor to bring Jesus to crucifixion.

That should have been the end of it. But, at the next great feast, Pentecost, his followers proclaimed that Jesus had risen – in his physical body – from the dead. They then went out into the world and preached with such conviction that within a decade the new religion of Christianity had permeated almost the entire Roman Empire.

In assessing miraculous events as reported in the New Testament, three elements need to be considered – the records, the truth or falsehood of the facts chronicled and their interpretation.

First, the records. Apart from a few fragments, the oldest New Testament manuscripts date back to about the fourth century AD and are copies of copies. Part of the work of textual scholars is to reconstruct the original texts by comparing and collating surviving manuscripts and eliminating the inaccuracies, additions and annotations of copyists. Mark's gospel was written about AD 65, approximately 30 years after the events recorded, Luke's probably about AD 70, Matthew's late in the first century and John's about AD 100. They were based on earlier written material, in turn collected from oral tradition and statements of eyewitnesses, contemporaries of Jesus. Mark probably

Right: the gospel writers. Mark's gospel was written about 30 years after the events it recorded, Luke's shortly after that; Matthew and John's gospels were probably written around the end of the first century. Were their memories hopelessly muddled after such a long time – or were the events they recorded too amazing to forget?

Below right: Peter raises the dead Tabitha; early Christian propaganda or literal truth?

Right: a conventional Nativity scene, complete with adoring magi and heavenly choir, typical of the Midrash, or embroidered scriptural commentary. Angels appearing to shepherds, and the star of Bethlehem are, say biblical scholars, attempts by the gospel writers to create an atmosphere appropriate for the birth of the Son of God. Yet, if that were the true identity of Jesus of Nazareth, why should 'signs and wonders' not have accompanied his birth?

Far right: Jesus walks on the water, while Peter begins to sink the moment he takes his eyes off Jesus's face. Is this another example of the Midrash style – or did Jesus hypnotise Peter, releasing paranormal powers?

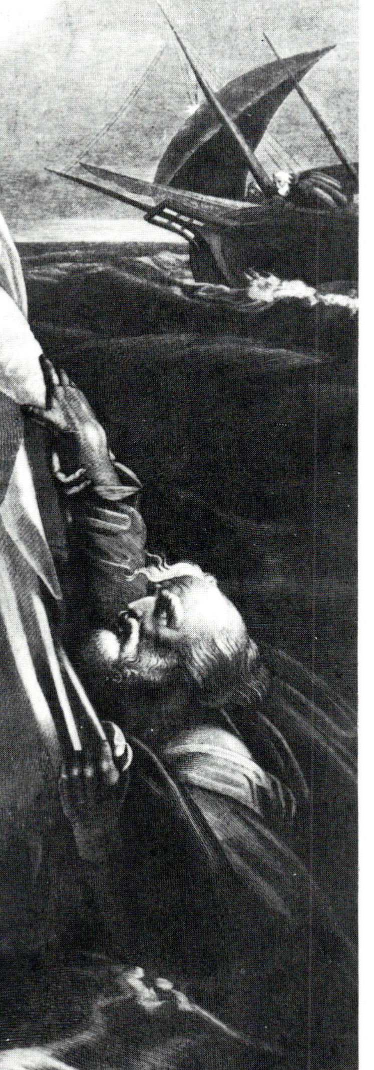

obtained information from Peter, leader of the Apostles, and Luke from Mary, Jesus's mother. Sceptics may therefore claim that the fallibility of memory and the unconscious exaggeration of each other's recollections by enthusiastic believers can explain away everything, and that records written so long after the events are worthless. Believers can argue that the records were based on the recollections of contemporaries of Christ, that events so astounding would imprint themselves upon the memory, that mere illusion could not have transfigured lives and made the impact on history that Jesus's career did, and that the most scholarly investigation by hostile critics has not succeeded in destroying the main fabric of the New Testament story, including its paranormal elements.

Star of wonder

In judging the records the writing conventions of the time must be considered. Ancient narratives were not as obsessed as 20th-century journalists with the literal accuracy of words and the reporting of events – the interpretation was more important than the happening, and their readers understood this. Thus Matthew, a Jewish Christian writing for Jews, used the technique of the Midrash, or embroidered commentary. This technique poetically and symbolically enhanced events that were, perhaps, wonderful in themselves, creating a suitable atmosphere to convey the wonder to the reader. So, the birth of Jesus was accompanied by the appearance of angels to shepherds, the star over Bethlehem and the visit of the wise men from the East. An earthquake, the rending of the

Temple veil, darkness and the appearance of spirits in the streets of Jerusalem signalled the death of Jesus. None of these events may have actually happened, but for all believers, what matters is not the physical events men experience but the spiritual experiences they symbolise.

Matthew also emphasises the fulfilment of prophecy, a favourite phrase being, 'that it might be fulfilled which was spoken by the prophets'. However, for 'fulfilled' read 'paralleled', for a rabbinical tradition was to quote Scripture as commentary; as when a rabbi, given a basin of oil in which to wash his feet, commented, 'that it might be fulfilled what is written in Deuteronomy, "let him dip his feet in oil"'.'Matthew never intended – any more than the rabbi – to state that the prophets foresaw the actual events.

Intervention of angels

Another Jewish convention is the device of ascribing the apparent intervention of God in the affairs of men to the action of 'an angel of the Lord'.

Prediction and precognition have a place in the New Testament but only, research reveals, as a matter of faith. Jesus predicted his death at Jerusalem at least three times. He prophesied the obliteration of the Temple, which occurred in AD 70. He foresaw Peter's denial of him. Agabus, a Christian prophet, warned Paul that the Jews of Jerusalem would deliver him to the Romans (Acts 21:9). But the records of these predictions were all written *after* their apparent fulfilment and are therefore useless as evidence for the power of prediction.

Mystical experiences, dreams and visions

abound. If the dreams of Joseph, Mary's husband (Matthew 1:20; 2:13; 2:19; 2:22), are not Midrashic, they can be accepted as dramatisations of solutions to problems of which he was aware when awake. Jesus, at his baptism, saw the heavens open, the Holy Spirit descending upon him like a dove and heard a voice saying, 'Thou art my beloved Son,' all of which was, apparently, personal to him. No bystander is reported as having seen or heard anything. Paul's conversion occurred when a light from heaven (lightning?) temporarily blinded him on a journey to Damascus and a voice addressed him. Acts 9:7 claims the voice was heard by Paul's

Below: an angel announces to Mary that she will bear the 'Son of the Highest'. The Holy Ghost is shown here as a dove – a symbol of God's especial favour – which is also mentioned in the New Testament description of Jesus's baptism (bottom)

Below right: Peter is freed from his chains by an angel. Is this an example of the Apostle's own PK ability activated by his dire need?

vision, sends for him. Peter, forbidden by Jewish law to enter a gentile's house, has a vision of creatures 'clean' and 'unclean'. Told to 'kill and eat', he replies that he has never eaten anything unclean. The reply comes, 'Do not call unclean what God has cleansed.' The vision coincides with the arrival of Cornelius's emissaries, and Peter, his scruples removed, visits Cornelius who is converted to Christianity – and the new faith is for the first time communicated to the gentile world (Acts 10).

The go-between

The psychical researcher can see in this story an unusual case of extra-sensory perception, the Roman's thoughts reaching out to the Jew and inspiring the reflection expressed in a vision that the whole of humanity was acceptable to God. But there is an extra dimension in that the communications are inspired by something or someone beyond the two men, an 'angel' who instructs Cornelius and a 'voice' that addresses Peter. Some parapsychologists, however, believe that this sort of disembodied voice may be an exteriorisation of one's own inner conviction – in effect, one literally hears not merely what one wants to hear but what one *needs* to hear. Thus the Apostles heard 'divine' voices at critical moments in their lives. Rex G. Stanford's theory of 'psi-mediated instrumental response' (PMIR) embraces the idea that prayers are answered, not by any outside agency, but by the person who prays, through the unconscious activation of a form of psychokinesis, but only when the need is greatest.

The delivery of Peter from prison, when he was sleeping chained between two guards, is frankly miraculous (Acts 12); but the story has a ring of truth about it and is paralleled in the similar release of a modern Christian, Sadhu Sundar Singh, in the early 20th

companions while Acts 22:9 denies this. The discrepancy cannot be denied – but neither can the fact that the arch-persecutor of the Christians became, as a result of his experience, their principal advocate. There is also a possible psychological explanation. Watching the heroic death of the first Christian martyr, Stephen (Acts 7), Saul – later Paul – was subconsciously convinced of the truth of Christianity. The conviction violently conflicted with his upbringing as a rigorous Pharisee, and the conflict had to be resolved by a cataclysmic personal experience.

More than psychology, however, is needed to explain the experience of Peter and Cornelius. Cornelius, a Roman centurion, given Peter's very name and address in a

century. This is only one of a number of biblical miracles that, although superficially incredible, can be matched by personal experiences today.

During Jesus's mission – a time of great spiritual outpouring – his followers may well have experienced the blossoming of psychic powers. If there is any truth at all in the strange experiences reported by saints and mystics down the ages, these continue to manifest in holy people. Many of the experiences, such as 'speaking with tongues', are explicable psychologically (see page 70), others, such as some of the well-attested healing miracles at Lourdes, are inexplicable.

At the same time a truly balanced view often actively cries out for a healthy and reasonable scepticism. Some of the miracles in the New Testament are ethically suspect – is the striking dead or blind of deceivers and

as such events can be; and there is no reason why Jesus's reputation as an exceptional healer should not be accepted at face value. His raising from the dead of Jairus's daughter (Matthew 9:18) – of whom he said, 'The maid is not dead, but sleepeth' – and of the widow of Nain's son (Luke 7:11-17) could both have been recoveries from comas. The raising of Lazarus (John 11) is a different matter. Not only is there here a man raised to life four days after his burial, but this astounding miracle – which finally decided the authorities to destroy Jesus – is ignored by the first three gospels. Yet the modern Hindu leader, Sai Baba, is also credited with raising from the dead a man whose body had actually begun to decompose.

But for Christians, there remains a miracle of raising that, if it happened, must be the most remarkable and significant event of all time: the physical resurrection of Jesus himself, three days after he died on the cross.

opponents, as Peter did to Ananias and Sapphira (Acts 5) and Paul to Elymas the sorcerer (Acts 13), albeit temporarily – reconcilable with Christ's teaching of 'Love thine enemies'? Was it ethical of the Lord of creation to send evil spirits into a herd of swine (Matthew 8) so that they were all drowned? (Although there is some evidence that this incident was misreported.)

Christians prefer to assess each miracle individually, according to its consonance with the true spirit of Christianity as they see it. Thus, Jesus's calming of the tempest at sea (Matthew 8:24) can be believed of a man so in tune with nature that he could read its signs, and his walking on the sea (Matthew 14:24) as an example of levitation – which has been reputed in different cultures and at different ages to be a property of holy men.

One outstanding characteristic of Jesus's life was his healing ability. The literature of the paranormal is crammed with stories of healing, many of them as well-authenticated

Bottom: Lazarus is raised from the dead. Some commentators suggest that Lazarus was in fact in a cataleptic trance, or a coma, and that Jesus, realising this, released him from the appalling fate of being buried – or entombed – alive. Yet in the 1970s, the Hindu leader Sai Baba is said to have 'raised' a man who had been dead for days and who had actually begun to decompose; perhaps Lazarus truly was dead when Jesus raised him

The gospel truth?

'The third day he rose again from the dead': thus the Christian creed asserts the miracle of Christ's bodily resurrection. But is this a religious myth – or a literal truth?

THE GREATEST MIRACLE – or the greatest illusion in history? Under which heading comes the resurrection from the dead of Jesus, called the Christ? The story is contained in all four gospels, and a reference to it in I Corinthians 15:3-7 probably embodies a creed dating from a period soon after Jesus's death. Here follows a summary of each account so they can be compared and contrasted.

Mark relates that Jesus was scourged and brutally treated by Roman soldiers, who buffeted him, crowned him with thorns and crucified him. He died at the ninth hour (3 p.m.) and had to be buried before the Sabbath began at 6 p.m., so that his corpse should not profane it. Joseph of Arimathea, a secret disciple of Jesus, boldly asked Pilate, the Roman governor, leave to bury the body. Pilate, surprised that Jesus was already dead, checked with the centurion in charge before granting Joseph's request.

Joseph wrapped the body in 'fine linen'

Below: the crucified Christ is lifted from the cross. The gospels tell of his suffering: he had been brutally scourged, crowned with thorns, nailed in hands and feet (above right) and pierced in his side – too much, surely, to survive by any normal means, especially in an age when medical care was primitive at best

(was this the Turin shroud? see page 39) and hurriedly laid it in a sepulchre hewn out of a rock, the entrance of which was blocked by a great stone. Mary Magdalene and Mary, mother of Jesus, noted where Jesus's body was laid.

Part of Friday, all of Saturday (the Sabbath) and part of Sunday, totalling about 36 hours, comprised three days according to Jewish reckoning. Very early on Sunday, Mary Magdalene, Mary the mother of James, and Salome went to the sepulchre to anoint the body properly with spices. They wondered who should roll away the stone from the tomb for them, and on their arrival were surprised to see a young man sitting there, clad in white. He said,

Be not affrighted: Ye seek Jesus of Nazareth, which was crucified: he is risen he is not here: behold the place where they laid him.

But go your way, tell his disciples and Peter that he goeth before you into Galilee: there shall ye see him, as he said unto you.

Terrified and bewildered, the women fled and told no one.

The risen Christ, Mark continues, appeared first to Mary Magdalene, who told the disciples and was not believed. Then he appeared 'in another form' to two disciples walking into the country, and finally to the 11 Apostles as they ate, reproaching them for their unbelief and exhorting them to preach

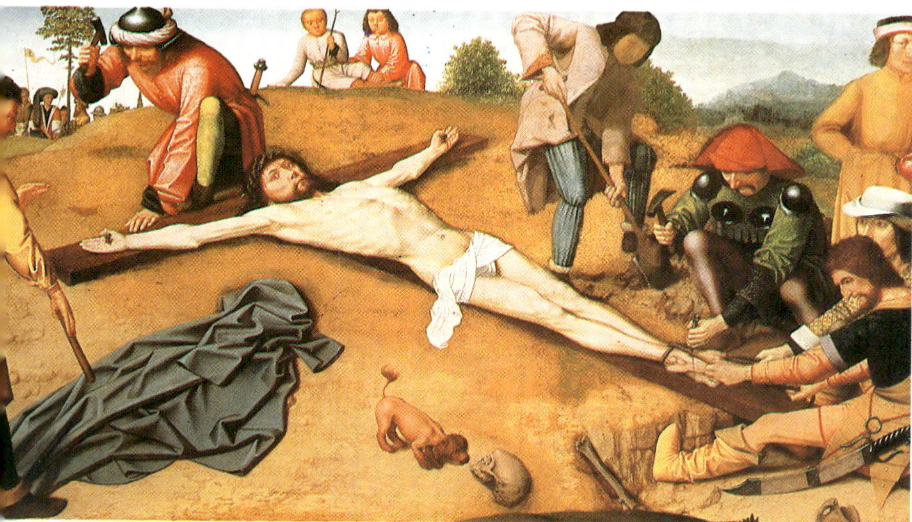

great joy, they run to tell the disciples. On the way there they are greeted by Jesus himself. He repeats the message that the disciples should go to Galilee where he and they will meet. Meanwhile the guards report what has happened to the chief priests, who bribe them to say that while they slept, the body was stolen by the disciples.

The disciples then meet Jesus as arranged on a mountain in Galilee, worshipping him – 'but some doubted' – and receive instructions to evangelise the world.

Luke asserts that the women (unnamed) not only beheld the sepulchre when Jesus was buried but 'how his body was laid'. On Sunday Mary Magdalene, Joanna, Mary the mother of James, and other women found the stone rolled away and were perplexed by the absence of the body. Suddenly, 'two men

the gospel throughout the world. Afterwards he 'was received up into heaven'.

Matthew adds a buffeting from the Sanhedrin (the Jewish council) to Jesus's other physical hurts. He also relates how the Jewish authorities, recalling Christ's claim that he would rise again after three days, asked Pilate to guard the body to prevent the disciples stealing it by night and claiming a miraculous resurrection. Pilate told them to use their own men, probably Jews from the Temple police, who kept order inside the Temple precincts where no gentiles were allowed.

Matthew omits Salome, mentioning only two women visiting the tomb at first light on Sunday. A great earthquake marks the descent from heaven of an angel with a face 'bright as lightning' and 'snow-white raiment', who rolls back the stone and sits upon it, terrifying the guards into stupefaction. He addresses the women in the same words as Mark's 'young man'. Filled with awe and

Right: a florid 19th-century depiction of Christ rising from his tomb, triumphing over death and corruption. On Pilate's orders a large boulder had been placed across the mouth of the tomb to ensure that the body could not be stolen, and its disappearance taken by Christians as evidence of the promised resurrection. But when some female disciples went to the tomb to anoint Jesus's body in the Jewish tradition, they found the boulder had unaccountably been rolled away, and a 'young man' was sitting there (below left). The gospels vary on this point: there are 'two young men', 'two angels', 'a young man' and 'an angel'. Whoever was sitting there was unknown to the women. According to Luke, the 'two men...in shining garments' said to the women: 'Why seek ye the living among the dead? He is not here, but is risen'

stood by them in shining garments' who gave them approximately the same message as reported by Mark and Matthew, adding a reminder that Jesus had prophesied his death and resurrection. The women told the disciples and were disbelieved, but Peter ran to the sepulchre, saw the discarded grave-clothes, and departed, puzzled.

Luke then describes the two disciples' walk to Emmaus, $7\frac{1}{2}$ miles (12 kilometres) outside Jerusalem. Jesus joined them but 'their eyes were holden that they should not know him'. They told him of the crucifixion and that certain women had found the tomb empty and had seen a vision of angels who affirmed that Jesus was alive. Other disciples visited the sepulchre and verified that the body was no longer there. Jesus expounded to them the scriptures 'concerning himself', was invited to share their evening meal and was recognised by them when, probably using characteristic gestures, he blessed and broke bread. Then he vanished from their sight. They returned post-haste to Jerusalem

and told the 11 Apostles, who reported in their turn that the Lord had appeared to Peter. While they were talking, Jesus appeared suddenly in their midst. Thinking they were seeing a ghost, they were terrified; but he invited them to touch him, showing them his wounded hands and feet and proving his material nature by eating before them. He told them to 'tarry in Jerusalem until power came upon them' – there is no mention of meeting in Galilee – and, leading them out of the city to Bethany, ascended from their sight 'into heaven'. The disciples remained joyfully in Jerusalem, worshipping daily in the Temple.

John adds that a soldier pierced Jesus's side with a spear while he was on the cross and that there came out 'blood and water', a medically accurate description of the piercing of the pericardium – a fatal wound if Jesus had not already died. John mentions a visit on Sunday morning 'while it was yet dark' of Mary Magdalene only. Seeing the stone rolled away, she ran to tell Peter and John that Jesus's body had been removed and 'we' (clearly indicating the presence of others with her) 'know not where they have laid him.' The two ran off together. John, outstripping Peter, looked into the sepulchre and saw the linen clothes lying there but remained outside. Peter pushed past him, John followed and, noting that the head-cloth was lying apart from the grave-clothes, they left, 'wondering'.

Mary Magdalene, returning to the tomb, stood outside it weeping and, stooping down,

Top: the resurrected Christ meets two disciples on the road to Emmaus, 'But their eyes were holden that they should not know him.' Seeing the risen Jesus as a stranger, the disciples told him enthusiastically of the resurrection. Later, when sharing an evening meal at Emmaus, the 'stranger' suddenly revealed himself as the risen Jesus (above). The real mystery is why no one recognised him

saw two 'angels' – whom she seems, nevertheless, to have accepted as normal human beings at the time, for when they asked her why she was weeping, she replied, 'Because they have taken away my Lord and I know not where they have laid him.' Turning, she saw Jesus but (perhaps because her eyes were dimmed with tears) did not recognise him. Mistaking him for a gardener, she asked him where he had put Jesus's body. He replied, 'Mary' – in such a way that she instantly recognised him. He told her not to touch him, but to tell the disciples that he was alive.

The same evening Jesus appeared among the disciples. Thomas, who was absent at the time, later refused to believe that Christ had been resurrected unless he could touch Christ's wounds. Eight days later Jesus appeared again, and Thomas was convinced.

Besides its innate improbability, the

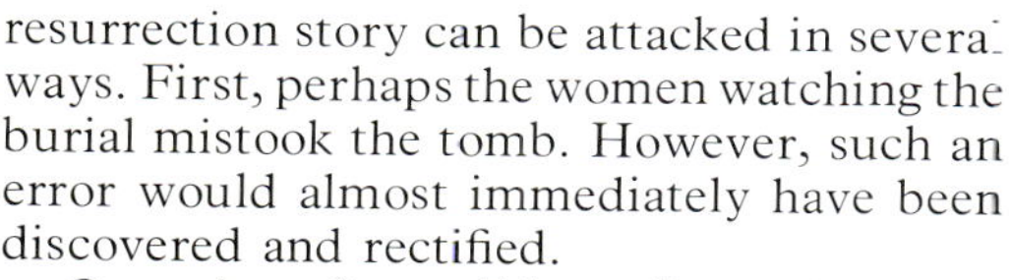

Left: the 'Holy Ghost' (or Holy Spirit) descends upon the Apostles at Pentecost, in the form of tongues of fire. The writers of the scriptures could well have been writing symbolically, but there is no reason why real tongues of fire should not have been the 'outward and visible sign of an inward and spiritual grace'

Right: not unnaturally, one of Jesus's disciples, Thomas, doubts that the abused and tortured Jesus could possibly have been resurrected. Understanding Thomas's scepticism, the risen Jesus prompts Thomas to feel the reality of the resurrected body, by probing the wound made by the centurion's spear

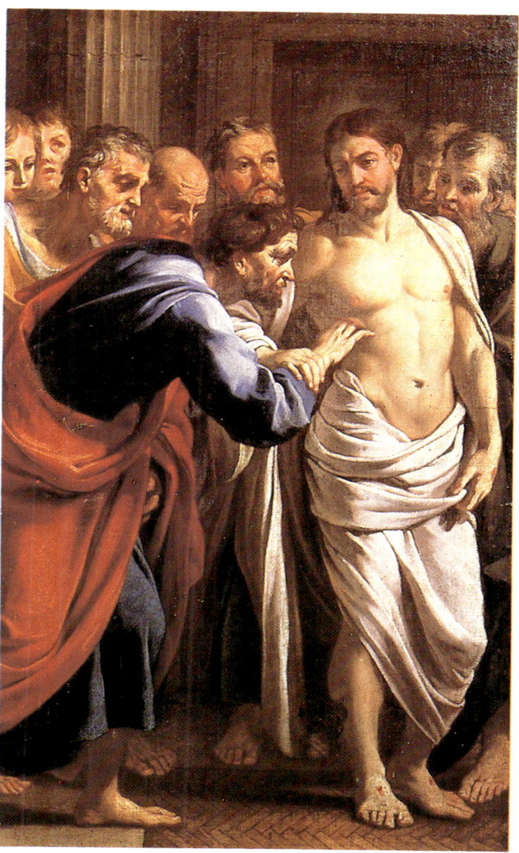

resurrection story can be attacked in several ways. First, perhaps the women watching the burial mistook the tomb. However, such an error would almost immediately have been discovered and rectified.

Or perhaps Jesus did not die on the cross, but only swooned, recovered in the tomb, escaped from it and was seen afterwards by one or two followers. A Roman scourging was so terrible that many victims died under it; even a short crucifixion could be fatal; the spear thrust in itself would have been lethal; the centurion – presumably experienced in such matters – confirmed Jesus's death. And how could Jesus have possibly escaped from the tomb after such ill-treatment?

Another explanation is that the body was stolen by some of the disciples who deceived the others into thinking Christ had risen. But it is highly unlikely that a religion that spread throughout the Roman Empire so rapidly, against intense persecution, could have been founded on a deception, especially as the leaders who presumably engineered the conspiracy themselves went heroically to martyrdom without one of them revealing the plot.

Or was the body removed by the Romans or the Jews, to nip Christianity in the bud? But in that case, why was it not produced the moment Christ's resurrection was begun to be preached? Or, if the body had been hidden in the wrong grave just a few minutes' walk outside Jerusalem, why was it never revealed? Peter's first preaching of the resurrection resulted in 3000 conversions – an unlikely outcome for a sermon based on a lie that could have been so easily exposed.

Critics point out that the gospel stories are full of discrepancies. However, this can be seen as a strength, as it shows there was no collusion among the writers. They also show

their confidence in their case by admitting, unnecessarily, details that weaken it, such as the temporary non-recognition of Jesus and their doubts. Moreover, the stories can be substantially reconciled, as a renowned scholar, N.P. Williams, has shown in his *The first Easter morning*. However, the events recorded in the New Testament may have been telescoped by writers whose conventions did not include rigorous adherence to chronology.

Of the nature of Christ's resurrection body, which could apparently materialise or dematerialise at will, psychical research perhaps has something to say. Matter through matter – the teleportation of objects and even people – is a well-attested phenomenon, common in reports of poltergeist cases and said to occur frequently at seances. And bilocation – the appearance of a live human being in two places simultaneously – has been reported in the lives of Sister Mary of Agreda and more recently, Padre Pio who died in 1968.

Believers may also find supporting evidence of the resurrection in the Turin shroud, while sceptics still maintain that some unknown, but rational, factor convinced the first disciples of something that simply never happened.

Yet the annals of psychical research and the archives of collectors of anomalous phenomena point to the reality of 'miracles' – so perhaps there is no reason to doubt that the miracles of the New Testament did happen exactly as recorded.

Visions of the Virgin

Right: Joan of Arc being inspired by an angel to lead the French to victory against the English. 'The Maid', as she was known, heard voices that urged her to forsake the normal life of a peasant girl and become a soldier – and on at least one occasion she claimed to have seen St Michael himself. Her voices, however, seemed to have let her down badly, for her victories were few and transitory – and she died horribly at the stake. For this reason many commentators have suggested that her inspiration was diabolical in origin

For centuries believers have reported having experienced a vision of the Virgin Mary – and miracles of prophecy and healing have followed. KEVIN McCLURE discusses the stories of some world-famous visions

HISTORY IS FULL of visions. Visions that have led great men to do great things, and evil men to do evil things. Visitations from non-material figures led Joan of Arc to fight for France, and allegedly caused the Yorkshire Ripper to murder prostitutes. A researcher who looks for long enough can find visions of almost every kind – angels, demons, cities, monsters, heaven, hell, elves, fairies, flying saucers, saints, lovers, the dead and dying, and many more. Most of these visions are unique; seen once only, or rarely repeated. They relate only to the person who sees them, or to the place where they are seen, or to an individual combination of circumstances that is unlikely ever to occur again. Such visions may be fascinating, but few conclusions can be drawn from cases that vary so widely.

There are, though, a very few kinds of vision that are reported again and again, and show marked signs of repetition and consistency. There may be a variety of reasons for this, but if a large number of unconnected individuals claim a similar experience, we must begin to take them seriously, and wonder whether there is more to it than

Above: the grotto at Lourdes, France, where Bernadette Soubirous (right) had a vision of a beautiful lady who later said: 'I am the Immaculate Conception.' The statue of the lady in the grotto, however, reportedly provoked Bernadette to comment that it bore little resemblance to her vision. Although Bernadette herself died in agony from a tubercular knee in 1879, Lourdes has become a place of pilgrimage and many alleged miraculous healings. The sick and dying flock in great numbers (top, far right) to bathe in the water of the Lourdes grotto

illusion or imagination. Does the figure or person that is reportedly seen have some independent reality of his or her own?

The vision most frequently seen and experienced in the Western world in the past 800 years is that of the Virgin Mary, the Mother of Christ. There have been numerous variations in detail – in age, exact appearance, clothing, and companions – but the overall picture is remarkably consistent. And consistent, too, are the reports of healing and prophecy that often accompany the visions. Clearly, a pattern has been established, and some elements of the reports must be seen as the consequence of expectation and belief. But it does seem that there may be more to it than that – certainly, people's lives have been changed, often for the better, by what is

said to have been seen.

The number of visions reported must run into thousands, and is constantly increasing. By presenting eight separate cases, some famous, some less so, that have occurred in Europe and the USA in the last 150 years, a general impression of this fascinating field, at least, will be given.

La Salette is a small village in the French Alps, in the region of Grenoble. Here, on 19 September 1846, something of a pattern was set for visions of the Virgin. Two children, 15-year-old Melanie Calvat and 11-year-old Maximin Giraud, tending their herd of cows in a remote spot, saw a weeping woman, who seemed to be resting on the bed of a dried-up stream. She rose and said, 'Why do you not come nearer my children? Be not frightened. I have come to tell you some great news.' The two children described the woman as utterly radiant, 'brighter than the sun, but not to be compared with it'. She wore a long, sequined, white robe, with a white, patterned scarf, a yellow apron, and white, pearl-studded shoes. She wore a cross on her breast that shone with its own brilliance. Rays of light darted from her. Overcoming their fear, the children listened to the radiant figure. She predicted famine, and illness before it; that the grape and potato crops would rot. She complained bitterly of the distress caused her by the sins of the people, and is said to have given secret information, which was passed to Pope Pius IX in 1850.

As was often the case, priests and people alike were unwilling to believe the children's story at first, and they suffered threats, persuasion and – apparently – physical injury. But they did not retract their claims, and argued plausibly for what they had seen. The stream the children had seen to be dry flowed with water the next day; but, as predicted, the potato crops failed, causing famine in France and Ireland; philloxera destroyed the vineyards. The claims of the children at La Salette have never been completely refuted.

Bernadette's lady

The events at Lourdes, where a 14-year-old girl experienced 18 visions of the Virgin, are far better known. Films, plays, books and television have dealt repeatedly with the story of the small French town that has become the centre of so many hopes – and, sometimes, of seemingly miraculous healings. The image of the religious peasant girl, Bernadette Soubirous, collecting driftwood, seeing the Virgin, speaking with her, and watching the healing spring bursting forth from the ground are now the stuff of legend. But we should look a little closer at the vision itself, through an English translation of Bernadette's own account:

I looked up and saw a cluster of branches and brambles underneath the highest opening of the grotto, tossing and swinging to and fro, although nothing else stirred.

Behind these branches and inside the opening, I saw at that moment a girl in white, no bigger than myself, who greeted me with a slight bow of her head. . . . She was wearing a white dress right down to her feet and only the tips of her toes were showing. The dress was gathered high at the neck from which there hung a white cord. A white veil covered her head and came down over her shoulders and arms almost to the bottom of her dress. On each foot I saw a yellow rose. The sash of her dress was blue and hung down below her knees. The chain of the

evening of 21 August 1879. The scene on the outer wall of the chapel in this remote village was described by the local *Tuam News*:

> The first person who saw it passed on, but others soon came and remained, and these saw covering a large portion of the gable end of the sacristy, an altar, and to its sides the figures of St John the Evangelist, the Blessed Virgin, and St Joseph .... the altar was surrounded by a brilliant golden light through which, up and down, angels seemed to be flitting .... To St John's right, the Blessed Virgin, having her hands extended and raised towards her shoulders, the palms of her hands turned towards the people, and her eyes raised up towards heaven .... These figures remained visible from 7.30 p.m. to 10 p.m., witnessed during that time by about twenty persons. . . .

Here, the Virgin is said to have worn a white

rosary was yellow, the beads white and big, and widely spaced. The girl was alive, very young and surrounded with light. When I had finished my rosary she bowed to me smilingly. She retired within the niche, and suddenly disappeared.

This was all the communication that took place during the first vision; not until 25 March 1858 did the figure pronounce itself to be 'The Immaculate Conception' – a description and doctrine, oddly enough, defined by the Pope only four years previously. The visions continued until 16 July 1858, although the first healing miracle apparently occurred as early as 7 April. Clearly some confusion has arisen as to facts. Bernadette declared the figure she saw was 'no bigger than myself' – that is, a child, far from full-grown. Also, Bernadette did not at first give the figure a religious title, but referred to it merely as 'Aquero', meaning 'this thing'. As she had contact with a priest who believed strongly in the vision at La Salette, it is perhaps not surprising that in time she identified the figure as Mary, and that history has turned the child seen by Bernadette into the full-grown Mother of Christ. But this does not detract from the significance of the original experience, nor from the healings that seem to have been a direct result of Bernadette's vision.

By the mid 19th century, visions of the Virgin were becoming increasingly common all over Europe. Away from the visions of mainland Europe – and different in other ways too – were the events at Knock, County Mayo in the Republic of Ireland, on the

Top: the gable end of the church at Knock, County Mayo in Eire, where a paranormal altar, surrounded by the figures of the Virgin and other saints, was seen in August 1879. The two-dimensional quality of the reported vision has led sceptics to suggest that the 'vision' was in fact the projected image of a magic lantern show

Above: Pope John Paul addresses the faithful at the new basilica at Knock in 1979

dress and golden crown.

The physical nature of the Knock visions – flat, two-dimensional against a wall, statue-like and motionless in all essentials, surrounded by light, and growing brighter as night fell – has led to suspicions that the 'vision' was in fact an image cast by a magic lantern, or even phosphorescent paint on the wall. However, these rationalisations would seem unlikely to fool so many people for so long; but no other wholly conventional explanation has been put forward. Whatever the vision may have been – and we shall almost certainly never know now – it was clearly believable and convincing for those who saw it, and it had a tremendous effect. It occurred at a time of poverty, hardship and dispute, and regardless of its source it met a need. The scene of regular papal visits, the shrine at Knock now attracts over a million visitors a year. The vision communicated nothing, but a 'limestone broth' was made of plaster from the church wall mixed with holy water; it was administered to the sick, and claims of its healing powers were frequent.

Of the eight visionary events reviewed in this series, the apparitions at Llanthony are perhaps the most outlandish, occurring as they did in an Anglo-Catholic religious community. There was clearly some expectation of contact with the Divine, and in several ways the events followed a pattern.

The Virgin comes to Wales

The apparitions occurred in the grounds of the monastery at Llanthony Abbey, Capel-y-Fin, Wales, between 30 August and 15 September 1880. The community was very varied in composition, and was founded and led by the eccentric and remarkable Joseph Leycester Lyne, known as Father Ignatius. Following the appearance of a ghostly sacrament to a Sister Janet that morning, in the twilight of the evening of 30 August 1880 four boys of the community, aged between 9 and 15, claim to have witnessed a vision of the Virgin.

A halo of glory shone out from the figure all around in an oval form. The form was of a woman, a veil hung over the head and face, the hands were both raised as if in blessing. It approached very slowly. Its appearance was like the pictures of 'The Immaculate Conception' . . . . They saw the beautiful form enter the hedge, and after remaining there in the light for a few minutes, passed through the bush and vanished.

On Saturday, 4 September, in response to the singing of the 'Ave Maria', a light in the same bush developed into 'the form of a woman surrounded by light . . . the face and head covered with the veil'. Then, 'In the light appeared the form of a man, unclothed save a cloth round the loins . . . as the forms met, both vanished.'

The climactic event of the series occurred

Above and right: the vision of the Virgin as it floated over the Coptic orthodox church of St Mary at Zeitoun, Egypt, in 1968

Below: Father Ignatius, present at Llanthony Abbey, Wales (bottom), when the Virgin is said to have appeared in 1880

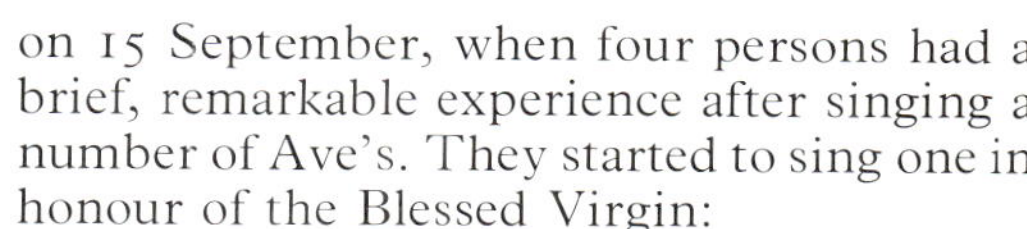

on 15 September, when four persons had a brief, remarkable experience after singing a number of Ave's. They started to sing one in honour of the Blessed Virgin:

> We had no sooner begun it than the whole heavens and mountains broke forth in bulging circles of light, circles pushing out from circles – the light poured upon our faces and the buildings where we stood, and in the central circle stood a most Majestic Heavenly Form, robed in flowing drapery. The Form was gigantic, but seemed to be reduced to human size as it approached. The figure stood sideways, facing the Holy Bush. The vision was most distinct and the details were very clear; but it was 'in the twinkling of an eye'.

Visions of the Virgin are rare in Britain and the accounts and claims of the Llanthony residents have been criticised – but they have never been disproved. There have also been reports of healing that was apparently effected with leaves of the Holy Bush, which is actually wild rhubarb.

The Virgin Mary, it is claimed, has appeared many times in the 20th century, mostly to children – and frequently bearing warnings of apocalyptic disasters to come. This chapter examines the background to these visions

THE VISIONARY EVENTS at La Salette and Lourdes in France, at Knock in Ireland and at Llanthony in Wales all happened in the 19th century. The first three sites have become major centres of pilgrimage, but Llanthony is nearly forgotten – perhaps because of inaccessibility, or because there is no Catholic tradition in Wales. In three of the reports it was claimed that healing accompanied the vision. Three of the cases prominently featured children. Two of the figures spoke and prophesied – two did not.

There are marked similarities among the descriptions of the figures in all these cases. And in all of them the experience is reported as having had a lasting effect on the witnesses.

The 20th century has seen no abatement in the frequency of visions, nor in their complexity; modern photographic and recording techniques have, in fact, made them much more thoroughly known by an eager audience of believers. Our second group of cases are spread even further geographically – from Spain to the United States – but they have many features that resemble those in the earlier reports. In all four, the visionary figure speaks, and in three there is extensive prophecy. The figure seen is apparently much the same in all the cases and healings

Out of the mouth of babes

One of the most famous modern visions was that at Fatima, Portugal, in 1917, in which three children, Jacinta, Francisco and Lucia (right), saw and spoke with 'the Lady of the Rosary'. Thousands of people witnessed extraordinary phenomena while the children apparently spoke to 'the Lady' every month for six months. Fatima is now a centre of pilgrimage (below)

are claimed in all of them. In the three major cases of the four, the original and prominent witnesses are children.

The apparently miraculous events at Fatima, Portugal, in 1917 are well-known, particularly for the 'Dance of the Sun' that ended the last vision in the series of six, and for the mystery surrounding the prophecies said to have been given by the Virgin to the young witnesses – Lucia dos Santos, aged nine, Francisco Marto, aged eight, and his sister Jacinta, aged six. They were looking after sheep just outside Fatima when they saw the apparition of a boy 'aged about 15' who exhorted them to pray. The 'angel', as they called him, appeared to them twice more that year, but it is the series of events that began on 13 May 1917 that has made Fatima world famous.

From out of a clear sky . . .

The three children were once again out tending their families' flocks when a flash of lightning – in a clear sky – sent them scurrying for shelter. But no rain came; instead they saw an apparition of a beautiful young woman, aged about 18. Lucia talked to her while Jacinta looked on. The vision said she had come from heaven and that she would reappear on the 13th of every month for a period of six months.

The children agreed that they would keep the story of the vision to themselves, but when they got home Jacinta blurted it out. The news predictably spread like wildfire, and soon crowds gathered outside Fatima on the 13th of every month.

The vision was seen – although only by the three children – every month from May to September, while the attendant crowds grew. On 13 October some 70,000 people were present when the phenomenon that came to be known as the 'Dance of the Sun' took place – although by no means all of them saw it. It has been described thus in a Catholic pamphlet:

> The rain stopped suddenly, and through a rift, or hole, in the clouds the sun was seen like a silvery disc. It then seemed to rotate, paused, and rotated a second or third time, emitting rays of various colours. Then it seemed to approach the earth, radiating a red light, and an intense heat. The crowd fell into a panic, thinking the world was ending, and then into tumultuous devotion.

It is unfortunate that the only photographs said to have been taken at this event appear to be fakes; certainly they are less than convincing.

The figure itself was described as: 'A beautiful Lady, who seemed to be less than 18 years old. She wore a white robe, and her head was covered with a white veil. Her hands, clasped in prayer, held a rosary.'

The matter of the prophecies is most intriguing. The first two, supposedly given

Above: pilgrims at the shrine at Beauraing, Belgium, which was built in the 1930s after five children (right) from two poor families claimed to have seen and spoken with the Virgin 33 times. Despite the number of alleged communications, the 'Lady' said little of any consequence. But even so, the story of the visions seems to have answered a deep need among Catholics, who flock to the shrine in great numbers

to the child Lucia in 1917, are the less convincing for being revealed *after* their alleged fulfilment, in 1936 and 1941, but the third prophecy of Fatima remains one of the great mysteries. Said to have been given to Lucia on 13 July 1917, it was passed in secrecy to the Vatican, and is said to have been opened in secrecy by the Pope in either 1942 or 1960. Contrary to Lucia's apparent instructions, no official information has been given as to what it contains, but journalists and religious extremists have made a variety of guesses.

Purportedly, it refers to appalling, worldwide war in the latter half of this century, to division within the Church, to the rise of Satan, and to the only gradual victory of Christ. There is a rumour that in 1977 Christ himself appeared to an anonymous Catholic to state that the secret 'must be known by all by now', and clearly there is a widespread feeling that the facts – if facts there be – are being wilfully withheld.

The visions at Beauraing, Belgium, which

also used as propaganda in battles in national and Church politics.

Thurston and Helle's description of the Lady is quite standard.

They saw her shining form as she stood on what appeared to be a small cloud. Her white dress seemed to be touched with reflections of blue light, and her hair was covered by a white mantle. From her head came short rays of light, which gave the appearance of a crown. Her hands were joined, and she was looking towards heaven.

One of the children claimed that the vision revealed her golden heart to her, but despite a continued stress on the significance of the Immaculate Conception, there was little meaning in what the figure had to say. Nonetheless, huge crowds were drawn who were prepared to accept the children's word about the vision, planted as it was firmly in

lasted from November 1932 to January 1933, introduced some new elements to the subject of the Marian visions. They were witnessed by, and only by, five children from two poor families, aged from 9 to 15. Thirty-three visions were said to have been seen and, although there was no independent verification, some of the visions were attended by very large crowds indeed. One fairly objective account tells of the first vision:

On 29 November 1932 four children at Beauraing went to meet a friend from her convent school. After praying in a Lourdes Grotto in the garden of the convent, one of them rang the doorbell. They all waited, expecting one of the sisters to open the door. Suddenly, as Andrée was looking towards the viaduct, she cried out, 'I see the light.' 'It must be the headlight of a car,' answered one of the other children. All looked in the direction of the source of the light. 'Something is moving there – is it a man or what?' they asked each other. Then Albert Voisin shouted, 'This is the Blessed Virgin.' All looked again, and all were convinced that it was the Blessed Virgin walking on the bridge. . . . This was the beginning of the 33 apparitions . . . at one time 30,000 people crowded around the site during the apparition, though only the children were favoured.

One of the new elements at Beauraing was the depth of investigation relating to the claimed visions – including tests of the children's trance state using lighted matches and a penknife that seem to have demonstrated genuineness. Lengthy, learned and unconvinced accounts of the events were recorded by the Catholic historians Herbert Thurston and Jean Helle. The visions were

Top: the valley in which lies the Spanish village of Garabandal where, in 1961, four young children (above) began to see visions of angels – which, they were told, heralded the vision of the Virgin herself. She is said to have appeared an astonishing 2000 times over a four-year period; sometimes she was accompanied by angels – and once by what the children described as 'the eye of God'. During their visions they became entranced, parading about in 'ecstatic marches' or falling backwards in perfect synchronisation. Yet one of the children, Maria Cruz Gonzales, has since confessed that some of her 'trances' were fakes

the tradition of Lourdes. Though independent commentators had serious doubts, and there was little objective evidence, believers continued to flock to Beauraing.

A series of visions more plausible to both the serious researcher and the Church commenced at Garabandal, a small village in north-west Spain, on 18 June 1961. Again, four young children, all girls aged 11 and 12, were the only witnesses to the Lady herself. She spoke at length and in detail, with prophecy and admonition. Astonishingly, the figure is said to have appeared to the children some 2000 times in four years. Considerable evidence exists of related healings – including one restoration of sight. The village has since become a major centre of pilgrimage.

The events commenced with nine appearances of an angel, warning the children that the Virgin would appear to them as 'Our Lady of Carmel'. Thus, even for the Virgin's first appearance, there were many witnesses present. 'Before the children . . . the Virgin appeared with two angels, one on each side.

Above the Virgin was a large eye that seemed to the children to be the eye of God.' They later described her:

> She has a white dress, a blue cape, a crown of golden stars. She holds between her fine slender hands a brown scapular [cloak] except when she carries the Child in her arms. She has long chestnut hair with a parting in the middle. Her face is oval with a very delicate nose, a very pretty mouth with well-traced lips. She appears to be 18, and is on the tall side.

The children, from their photographs, look cheerful and sensible enough. Yet while they saw the visions and spoke with the Lady, countless numbers of pilgrims and others watched them, and the doctors and investigators got on with their own peculiar duties. But the children seem to have been in genuine ecstatic trances, and were oblivious

Since 1970 Veronica Leuken, the 'Bayside seeress' from New York, has claimed she has had visions of the Virgin, who blessed her Polaroid camera so that it takes pictures with strange effects (bottom), especially the appearance of the so-called 'Ball of Redemption' (below). Critics, however, think it resembles a thumb over the lens. Veronica claims the Virgin imparts warnings and prophecies concerned with the laxity of morals in the modern world and the threat of 'satanic' influence on the Church. But no known prophecies concern specific events

however, have always maintained that their visions and trances were genuine.

This is not the place to enter into a detailed discussion of the various cases of visionary experience we have considered. A number of the arguments for and against accepting them at face value will have become apparent, as, too, will have the very simple beginnings onto which faith, enthusiasm, need and hardship have grafted a complex and dramatic superstructure in cases such as Lourdes and Beauraing. The consistent and yet inconstant appearance of the Virgin herself – changing in age, perhaps according to the age of the witness, and changing in title and characteristics according to the need and the situation – gives an impression that the visions may be only different versions of a similar psychological archetype; there may be no objective reality to all or any of the figures. But against this we have to balance the fact that most of the visions have been seen by unsophisticated, young children, apparently unprompted; can we really expect them to come up with such consistent, sophisticated stories? Also there is the matter of the many healings, and the prophecies – can a psychological illusion have such effects? Can it prophesy future events in detail and, as at La Salette, with accuracy?

Of course, there are no simple answers. But the evidence of thousands of witnesses points to the fact that something unusual has occurred at such places as Fatima and Lourdes – perhaps they were genuine visitations from Mary, the Mother of Christ. Certainly until we have a great deal more evidence – evidence we may never obtain – we are in no position to decry or dismiss any sincerely held belief based on these undoubtedly inspiring experiences.

to intrusions into their communication. They were apt to fall backwards (as do many subjects of conversion, faith healing and exorcism), sometimes together as if synchronised, or to link arms and parade backwards and forwards in 'ecstatic marches'.

The messages were similar to those given at Fatima. They consist mainly of threats, warnings and expressions of concern. A sequence of events is outlined: that there will first be a warning, of which everyone on Earth will be aware, then a miracle will occur at Garabandal – of which Conchita, one of the witnesses, now living in the USA, will give eight days' warning. As a result of this miracle the USSR will be converted wholesale to Christianity, and a 'permanent supernatural sign will remain until the end of time'. If the world does not then repent, the chastisement will follow.

Unfortunately, one of the children, Maria Cruz Gonzales, has since told interviewers that some of their 'ecstasies' were certainly faked, adding that they used them as a ruse to get away from the town to play. The others,

A shower of roses

When an obscure Carmelite nun died at the age of 24 in 1897 no one could forsee her popularity as a saint. PIERS CROKE describes the life of St Thérèse of Lisieux — and the miracles associated with her

AS ZELIE GUERIN WAS CROSSING the bridge over the river Sarthe at Alençon in northern France one blustery day in October 1858, she saw a strange man walking towards her – and, according to her own account, a voice within her told her, 'This is he for whom I have prepared you.'

His name was Louis Martin, a watchmaker in the town. The couple fell into conversation, an exceptional event, for both were modest and pious to an unusual degree, and found they had a great deal in common. Both were the children of army captains who had served under Napoleon. But even more

Below: the main street of Alençon in northern France as it was in the late 19th century. It was here that Zélie Guérin and Louis Martin were first drawn to each other, apparently by the hand of God. They married and had a large family; all the boys died in infancy and all the girls became nuns – among them the future saint

Right: Sister Thérèse in the convent garden, holding a lily – traditional symbol of virginal purity

remarkably, both had at one time felt religious vocations, but had been frustrated in achieving them. Zélie had sought admission to the Sisters of St Vincent de Paul, and had been turned down without explanation. Louis's earnest efforts to become a monk at the Grand St Bernard Abbey had come to nothing when he was unable to gain a sufficient mastery of Latin.

Within three months, the couple were married. By their own choice, it was a marriage of perfect monastic chastity. For 10 months, they lived happily as brother and sister, until Louis's father confessor, no doubt feeling that such a state was unnatural, advised them that it was God's will that they should have children. Louis and Zélie took him at his word, and over the next 14 years they produced five girls and four boys. The boys all died in infancy, but the five girls

Many miracles have been ascribed to St Thérèse, whose popularity shows no sign of diminishing. Votive candles offered in the hope of her direct intercession burn brightly (above) in the great Basilica at Lisieux (left), which has gradually become a place of pilgrimage

survived to succeed where their parents had failed in entering monastic life. And the most devout of them, Thérèse, was canonised a saint of the Roman Catholic Church in 1925, a mere 28 years after her death.

Zélie died from breast cancer when Thérèse was four years old, but the little girl's childhood in the old stone-built town of Alençon was nevertheless unusually happy. Her father called her *ma petite reine* ('my little queen') and would deny her nothing – to the extent that a less exceptional child might have been spoilt. This point did, indeed, later occur to the Promoter of the Faith appointed by the Pope to investigate the case for Thérèse's canonisation. But he found no evidence to suggest that she was other than a delightful and lovable child.

Not surprisingly, given the pious environment in which she grew up, she was a devout Catholic from her earliest years. She was later to write in her autobiography, *Histoire d'une âme*, that 'from the age of three I denied God nothing.'

The Promoter of the Faith did, however, find one fault in her character: a marked obstinacy of spirit – which was said to be

successfully curbed except when Thérèse believed she was prompted by the will of God. It was in this way that she was to justify a dramatic breach of etiquette she committed during an audience with the Pope in 1887.

In that year, the Bishops of Normandy sponsored a public pilgrimage to Rome – a rare event. Thérèse, by now 14 years of age, had a particular reason for wishing to join it. Her three elder sisters had already become nuns and it was her fervent desire to follow them within the next year. Not unreasonably, the ecclesiastical authorities rejected her request to become a novice on the grounds of her extreme youth. For Thérèse, however, this was merely a bureaucratic obstacle in the path to which God had called her, and she determined to seize the chance to make a direct appeal to the Pope, Leo XIII. To the alarm of the clerics in charge of the pilgrims, she made no secret of her intentions. The priests told her firmly to hold her tongue, an order that was reinforced in the very ante-chamber of the papal audience hall. Nevertheless, when her turn came to kiss the Holy Father's extended hand, she grasped it and tried to present her case. Two of the Pope's helmeted Swiss Guards at once stepped forward to remove her. But, recovering from his astonishment, the Pontiff allowed her to continue, although his answer to her request was diplomatic: 'Well, you will enter the convent if it is God's will . . .'

Silence and scourges

So, astonishingly – and against all precedent – the authorities in France relented and Thérèse was received into the Carmelite Convent in Lisieux the following year. The regime of the order was harsh even by the standards of the day. The nuns ate no meat, and from September to Easter took only one meal a day. From rising at 4 a.m. till rest at 10 p.m., most of the time was spent in complete silence. In addition, each nun was required to scourge her naked body several times a week with a *disciplina*, a sort of cat-o'-nine tails made of knotted leather thongs.

Thérèse accepted the daily suffering humbly and thankfully for the glory of God. Discussing the use of the scourge, her younger sister Céline confessed to her that she 'stiffened involuntarily in an effort to suffer less.' Thérèse expressed surprise: 'I whip myself in order to feel pain, as I want to suffer as much as possible. When the tears come into my eyes, I endeavour always to smile.' Later, however, she came to reject the use of instruments of mortification, emphasising instead the importance of complete obedience to God in every aspect of life.

Thérèse's devoutness and cheerfulness were exemplary, and remarked by everyone who knew her. In recognition of these qualities, she was entrusted, at the age of 23, with the care and training of novices. Then, one morning, she suffered a severe haemorrhage. The privations of her life had taken

The making of a saint

The process leading to the canonisation of Roman Catholic saints is a lengthy and rigorous one. The bishop of the diocese in which the candidate lived holds an enquiry and sends the results to Rome. Here, the case is put into the hands of a committee known as the Congregation for the Causes of Saints. The Congregation appoints two men to examine the case further: the Postulator of the Cause, who argues for the case, and the Promotor of the Faith – commonly known as the Devil's Advocate – who searches out reasons why the candidate should not be canonised.

The life and claims to holiness of the candidate are now examined; in the case of non-martyrs, two well-attested miracles are required for the initial step of beatification, which takes place before canonisation. A five-man committee is appointed by the Congregation to examine the case in greater detail; if it is successful, it goes back to the Congregation for discussion at three consecutive meetings. The Pope himself attends a final meeting and if, after 'prayerful consideration', he supports the cause, yet another meeting is held. The Pope can now declare the candidate blessed.

The final step in the process takes place if a further two or more well-authenticated miracles are proved to have taken place through the intercession of the person declared blessed. These are discussed at three meetings of the Congregation; a final meeting is held, and the Pope issues a document known as a *Bull of Council*, in which he states that the new saint is worthy of honour and imitation by the whole Church.

their toll. Tuberculosis was diagnosed, and she was given a year to live.

Towards the end, in 1897, she remarked to one of the nuns who tended her, 'I have never given God anything but love and is it with love that I will repay. After my death I will let fall a shower of roses. Now I am in chains like Joan of Arc in prison, but free soon, then will be the time of my conquests.'

The infirmary sister, no doubt thinking to humour her, replied, 'You will look down from heaven.' 'No,' answered Thérèse vehemently, 'I will come down.'

On her deathbed she was brought roses. Deliberately removing the petals one by one, she touched them to a crucifix beside her bed. A few fell to the ground, and seeing this she cried earnestly, 'Gather them carefully! One day they will give pleasure to other people. Don't lose a single one of them.'

The final death agony was a long one. For hours Thérèse fought for breath, her hands and face turning purple, her mattress becoming soaked with sweat. To add to her pain, the doctor's prescription of morphia was denied her by an eccentric and tyrannical Mother Superior.

Many Roman Catholics believe that Thérèse's sufferings were not in vain. After her death there occurred a remarkable series of phenomena – miracles? – many of them connected with the rose whose petals she plucked when she was dying. Whether or not the rose is responsible, as some people think, these events defy rational explanation.

Take the case of Ferdinand Aubry. A man of 60, he was admitted in 1910 to the hospital of the Little Sisters of the Poor in Lisieux for treatment of ulcers of the tongue. His condition deteriorated rapidly, and gangrene set in, causing the tongue to split and then fall apart. Medical opinion gave the man only a few days to live. In desperation, the Sisters begged one of Thérèse's rose petals from the nearby Carmelite convent. Ferdinand was induced to swallow it. The following day, he was cured. His tongue, however, was so badly damaged that it took the nuns some minutes to interpret his first attempts at speech to mean, 'When will my tongue come back?' Sadly, they shook their heads. But three weeks later, as contemporary photographs attest, Ferdinand's tongue was restored, whole and entire.

A year earlier, a Scotswoman, Mrs Dorans, had been admitted to a Glasgow hospital with an abdominal tumour. Having taken no food for 10 weeks, she was failing fast. Her doctor, indeed, gave her just days to live. Then prayers were offered to Thérèse for her recovery by the local Catholic community. On the night when doctors expected

Below: Thérèse aged 15 with her widower father, just before she became the youngest nun in the Carmelite convent at Lisieux. M. Martin adored Thérèse, but her ardent sense of vocation convinced him that he should allow her to become a nun

Right: Thérèse lies dying in 1897. The privations of her religious life took their toll, but she 'offered up her sufferings to God' and pledged to return from heaven to help the faithful. She said that her death was only the beginning of her 'real work'

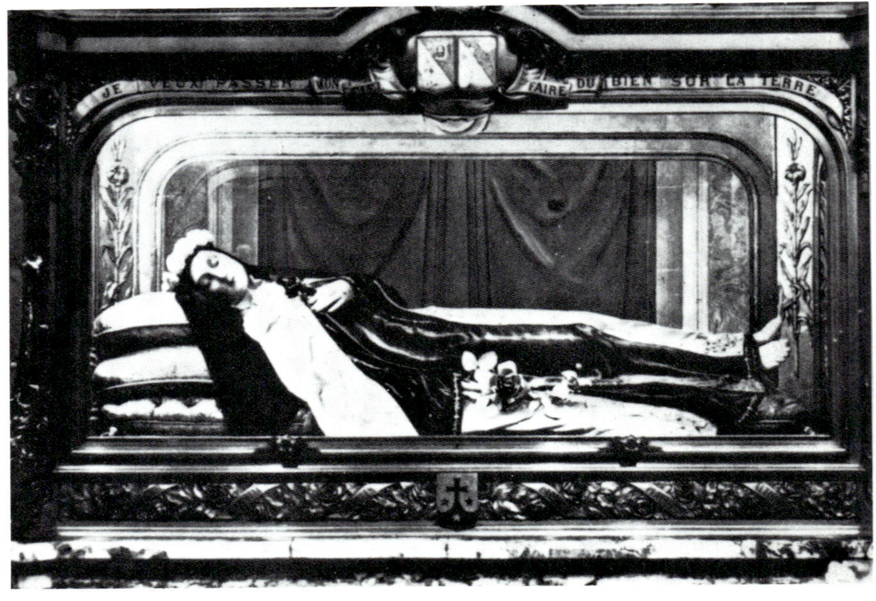

Bottom: a statue of the dead saint in the Basilica at Lisieux

her to die, Mrs Dorans felt 'a light touch on her shoulder', although there was no one in the room apart from her sleeping daughter. She fell asleep herself – to wake at 5.30 a.m., demanding tea and rolls. Later, doctors who examined her discovered that the tumour had regressed spontaneously, leaving a harmless lump the size of a marble.

A gardener's wife, Madame Jouanne, was rushed to a Paris hospital with peritonitis in 1912. She was operated on immediately, but so much pus was found when her stomach was opened up that she was immediately sewn up and simply left to die. But the priest who came to give her the last rites slipped a little silk purse containing one of the miraculous rose petals under her pillow. It seemed to succeed where medicine had failed, for Madame Jouanne made an instant recovery. She left hospital a week later and lived for many years afterwards.

A worldwide conspiracy?

Comparable stories of the intercession of Thérèse have subsequently been gathered from Austria, Belgium, Spain, Switzerland, Italy, Africa, the United States, Canada and China. The authenticity of many of the cases is unquestionable – unless, as one writer put it, one is 'prepared to believe in a worldwide conspiracy of priests, nuns, doctors and men and women of every rank and condition'.

A mere 20 years after her death, the Church acceded to the tumultuous clamour that Thérèse be officially venerated as a saint, and the process of investigating her case began. Contrary to popular opinion, this process is, in modern times, a rigorous one. At least four miraculous cases must be proved to the satisfaction of a panel of medical specialists. We have space to put forward just two of the cases. Sister Louise de St Germain was considered to be dying of a stomach ulcer. On the night of 10 September 1915, she dreamt that Thérèse appeared to her and promised her recovery. When she woke next morning, her bed was surrounded by rose petals – and no one could explain how they got there. Her condition, however, grew worse until the morning of 25 September, when she awoke to find herself completely recovered. Her cure is certified by a series of x-ray photographs.

Charles Anne was studying for the priesthood at Bayeux when, in 1906, he contracted tuberculosis. It had spread to both lungs, and he had had a number of severe haemorrhages. The case being pronounced beyond the scope of earthly medicine, he was persuaded to wear around his neck a silk purse containing some of the saint's hair. He tells of his forthright prayer to Thérèse: 'I did not come to this seminary to die: I came to serve God. You *must* cure me.'

The next morning, his prayer was answered. He was cured from that day on. The doctor in attendance affirmed the cure to be 'absolutely extraordinary and inexplicable from a scientific point of view'.

What distinguishes the miracles associated with Thérèse from those of many other saints of the Roman Catholic Church is that they occurred in our time and have been submitted to scientific scrutiny. Pope Pius XI and his cardinals needed little time to assess the evidence presented to them by their expert panel. In each of the cases examined, the evidence cited was incontrovertible. Let us end with the words used in the Apostolic Decree proclaiming the sanctity of Thérèse of Lisieux: 'Each instance involved the healing of an organic malady, one produced by pathological and anatomical lesion rigorously determined . . . such that the forces of nature . . . could not heal.'

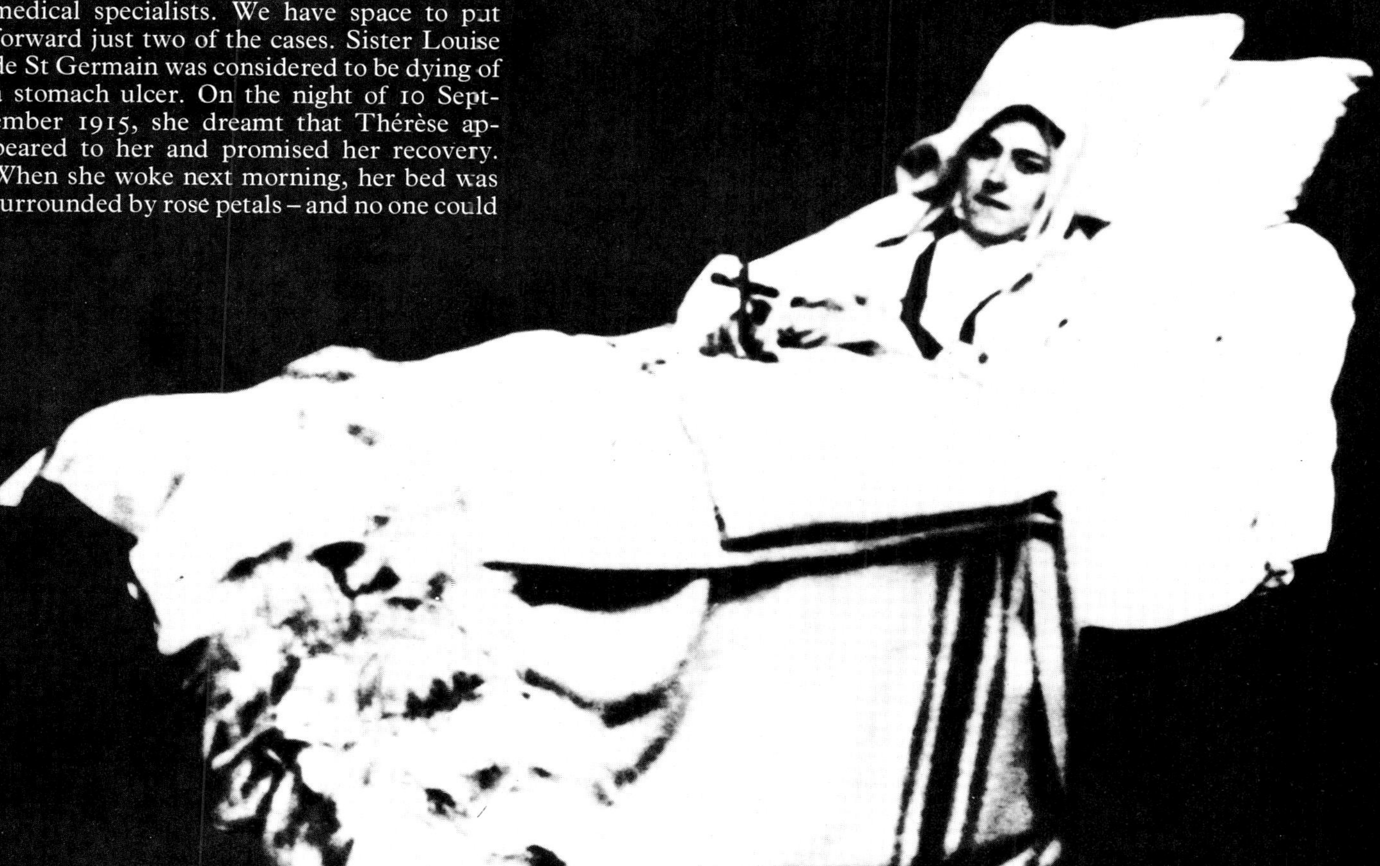

Tongues of men, or of angels?

Few expressions of religious ecstasy are as dramatic or as bewildering as 'speaking in tongues'. DAVID CHRISTIE-MURRAY examines this bizarre – yet surprisingly common – phenomenon

Above: religious emotion overcomes one member of the congregation during a service at a 'Holy Roller' church in the 1950s. The other members are unembarrassed: their church regards such displays of emotion as perfectly natural

Left: black Pentecostalists reach a crisis of religious fervour. When the ecstasy is at its height speaking in tongues may occur – and is taken as proof of the presence of the Holy Spirit

THE SCENE IS SET for an extraordinary – but by no means rare – phenomenon: the Pentecostalist minister's prayers grow more fervent; the congregation's responses correspondingly increase in enthusiasm. Cries of 'Glory be to God!', 'Jesus, blessed Jesus!', and 'Hallelujah!' resound through the church. A woman rises from her seat. Her voice swells until it drowns all the others, which sink into a chorus of soft murmurings. She begins to pour out a stream of completely unintelligible sounds – yet it is clearly a passionate paean of praise for the Lord. Then minister and congregation join in exalting the Holy Spirit of God who has granted their sister the gift of 'speaking in tongues'.

This phenomenon can be witnessed by anyone who visits a Pentecostalist church – although he may have to attend more than once as it does not automatically occur at every service.

'Speaking in tongues' nowadays implies speaking in *unidentified* tongues (or *glossolalia*). Before they could be recorded on tape, 'tongues' were often considered to be real, if unrecognised, human languages both ancient and modern (such as Incan and Eskimo), or perhaps even the 'tongues of angels' mentioned by St Paul in 1 Corinthians 13:1.

But since the advent of tape recorders and computers not a single case of *xenolalia* (paranormal speaking in real languages) has been recorded; the sounds that pour out so fervently at the Pentecostalist services have been proved not to be languages but language-types. A linguistics expert can tell the difference between glossolalia and xenolalia by analysing the structure of the 'tongues' spoken. He does not need to have a personal knowledge of every language, for the rule, to the expert, is quite simple – languages follow set laws and language-types do not. All the recorded 'tongues' have neither vocabulary nor syntax and so it must be concluded that Pentecostalist 'tongues' are neither the language of men nor, supposedly, that of angels. Although speaking in 'tongues' has been called 'refined gobbledygook' it is nevertheless a genuine form of worship. It seems that this bizarre phenomenon enables people

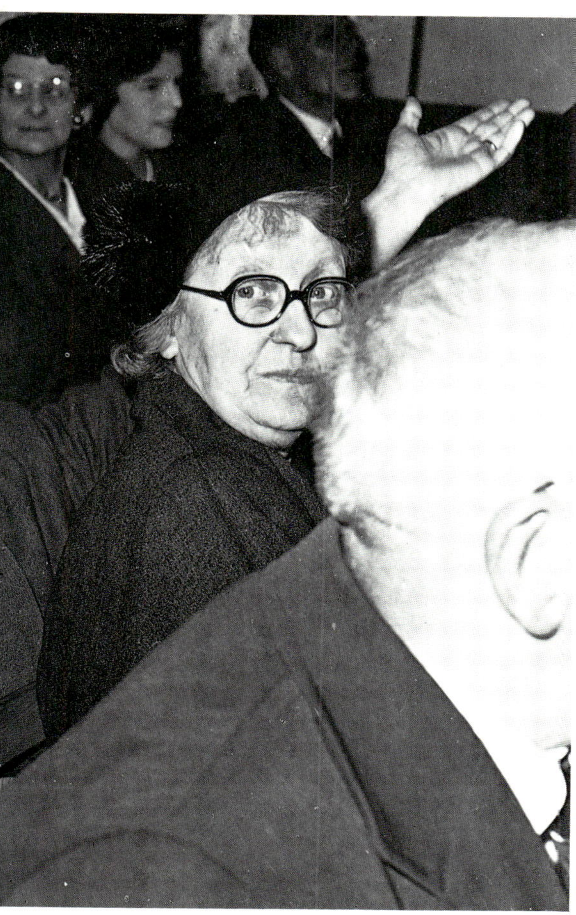

who normally lack the ability to express themselves in public to give vent to their religious emotions in such a way as to convince themselves and their fellow worshippers that the Holy Spirit is among them It uplifts the congregation and gives the speaker a sense of euphoric psychological release. But this form of communication by its very nature is emotional rather than educational, a sharing of mood rather than a conveying of information.

However, in almost every such congregation there is at least one 'interpreter of tongues' who speaks after the glossolalist and often sincerely believes that he or she is translating the 'tongues' into the vernacular. Although the interpretation itself can help to reinforce the ecstatic mood of the congregation it cannot be a translation or paraphrase of a language that does not exist.

Many Pentecostalists would deny that xenolalia has never been known in their churches, rightly pointing out that only a tiny percentage of all 'tongues' has ever been recorded or analysed. They also tell stories of numerous occasions when a foreign unbeliever, a casual visitor to the church, has been converted – by being preached at in his own language. This 'miracle' convinced the foreign sinner of the need to repent and join the Lord's church. Sometimes such a tale is told by the convert himself, sometimes by those who witnessed the alleged conversion. And since religious people are supposedly truthful, can all these reports be false?

The objective researcher must keep an open mind until he has at last captured on tape a translatable language – a recorded speech or speeches uttered at a service where a foreigner who spoke that language was present and to whom the message was relevant. The speaker must also be investigated to make sure that he was not normally fluent in that language, had never been exposed to it and had no prior knowledge that the foreigner would visit his church. But so far no such investigation has taken place.

Speaking in tongues among Christians first happened, so the New Testament tells us, when the disciples gathered in Jerusalem for the annual Jewish feast of Pentecost. This occasion was just seven weeks after Christ's crucifixion. The story is told by Luke (also author of one of the gospels) in Acts 2.

The disciples were worshipping at the Temple in Jerusalem, mingling with Jews from all over the known world, when they suddenly were seized by an ecstasy, caused by the conviction that Christ had risen from the dead. The 'Holy Ghost' is said to have descended on them, bestowing on them the 'gift of tongues' so that they shouted aloud their praise of God in all the languages of the visiting worshippers, to the great astonishment of the crowd.

But objectively the source of their xenolalia is not hard to pinpoint. Jewish religious law made attendance at certain festivals compulsory for every male adult Jew, but made allowances for great parts of the services to be spoken in the various vernaculars of the visitors present. So the disciples would often have heard what was recognisably praise of God in many languages, which they did not understand but which they probably stored deep down in

Below: an 11th-century Greek Orthodox mosaic showing the Day of Pentecost. Jesus's disciples are said to have been baptised by tongues of fire, which released such an ecstasy that they shouted praises of God in many languages unknown to them. This was the first instance of Christian 'tongues'

Left: a 16th-century stained glass window showing the conversion of St Paul on the road to Damascus. He warned against attaching too great a significance to 'tongues of men and of angels'

mainly drawn from ethnic minorities and poor people, and it was tainted at first – as its own historians admit – by hysterical behaviour and fanaticism. But it was a fast-growing movement and quickly spread throughout the world: it is by now by far the strongest Protestant group throughout predominantly Catholic South America, and surprisingly numerous even in countries such as Italy and Portugal, as well as in Protestant lands like Sweden. But today Pentecostal conduct and beliefs are more moderate, and in some of their churches the emphasis on 'tongues' is not as great as it was originally. 'Tongues' tend to be used more in private than in public worship these days. But possibly a much more important development of the use of glossolalia than the spread of Pentecostalism is the Charismatic Movement, which has affected almost every Christian denomination today. Small groups in individual Anglican, Baptist, Methodist, Presbyterian and even Catholic churches now meet to worship God in private, using

their subconscious minds. Moreover, Christ had promised to send them his 'Comforter' – whoever or whatever that might be – specifically at the feast of Pentecost. This heightened sense of expectation together with their conviction that Christ had risen could have resulted in the first Christian 'tongues'. (The account does not claim that the disciples understood what they were saying, nor does it mention that their utterances contained any specifically Christian message – it simply states that it happened, and astonished their fellow worshippers.)

The disciples' experience at Pentecost might have been considered unique in the annals of the Christian Church had it not been for St Paul's statement in 1 Corinthians 12–14 that 'tongues' were considered part of the normal worship of the Church at Corinth and that he himself was a glossolalist. Whether the Corinthian mode of worship was typical of that of the early Church is debatable, but – despite Paul's warnings against abuses of 'the gifts of the Spirit' (especially the misuse of 'tongues') and his stress on the 'more excellent way' of Christian love – these references to Corinthian glossolalia have been taken by some sects as a sacred mandate to use 'tongues' as proof of 'baptism by the Holy Spirit'.

Since the early days of the Church the use of 'tongues' has not always found favour among Christians. The Roman Catholics banned it from about the end of the first century – and later regarded speaking in 'tongues' as a sign of possession (except in the case of certain saints). Mainstream Protestantism also found no place for it. However it was kept alive down the centuries through fringe movements and heretical sects until, in the 20th century, it became the focal point for Pentecostalism. This movement started humbly, its members being

Above: a Christian convert emerges from a baptism by total immersion, crying aloud with joy. Often the climax of such baptisms results in 'tongues' being spoken by one or more of the participants

'the gift of tongues'. Unlike the humble members of the original Pentecostal Church, the members of the Charismatic Movement tend to belong to the professional middle-classes – and they use 'tongues' in private, in quiet, unemotional prayer. Such people do not regard 'tongues' as being real foreign languages, but take them rather as a sign of the Holy Spirit's revitalising effect upon the Church, often enabling the individual members to express the inexpressible.

The use of strange 'languages' is not exclusive to the Pentecostalists nor the Charismatic Movement, however. Since the foundation of modern Spiritualism about 130 years ago, hundreds of claims of spoken and written xenolalia by sensitives and psychics have been made.

Strange ecstatic speech

Instances of speaking in tongues have been recorded over centuries – but what causes these strange outbursts? This chapter investigates the phenomenon and examines the claims made for it

SPEAKING IN TONGUES – specifically in the languages of ghosts, ancestors, spirits, gods and totem animals – still features in the repertoire of shamans (tribal holy men) and medicine men in primitive societies the world over. In fact, no technique of 'supernatural' communication is more widespread.

There is a sense of poetic justice in the example of the African Zar spirits who 'afflict' women in male-dominated tribes with psychosomatic illnesses. The victim of the possession is a woman and the 'interpreter' – or exorcist – is also a woman. The exorcist addresses the Zar spirit in its own esoteric language, which cannot be understood without her interpretation. The Zar demands splendid clothes, perfumes and other luxuries through the lips of its victim; demands duly interpreted to the possessed woman's husband through the exorcist for a suitable fee. The sick woman will become well again – provided the spirit's requests are granted.

The position of shamans in their societies roughly corresponds to that held by priests and saints of old in the Christian world. From the end of the first century AD an ordinary Christian talking in 'tongues' would have been at best exorcised, at worst executed for 'trafficking with the Devil'. But saints were safeguarded, even as proven glossolalists, by their holiness. St Pachomius, an Egyptian abbot, claimed to talk to angels and wrote in a mystic alphabet understandable only to those in a special state of grace and similarly blessed. The German St Hildegard (1098–1179) spoke and wrote – in an unknown alphabet – an unknown language, which she translated into German. Specimens of it were preserved, published and analysed – and turned out to be a jumble of German, Latin and garbled Hebrew.

Bewitched by a priest

When the Ursuline nuns of Loudun in France became 'possessed' in the 1630s as a result of being bewitched by their curé, Urbain Grandier, they began to babble in 'tongues', allegedly recognised as Latin, Greek, Spanish, Italian, Turkish and even a Red Indian language. The sisters were certainly hysterical, and most modern accounts of the Loudun 'possessions' ascribe them to nothing more than sexual frustration.

Glossolalia became common after the Reformation – although neither Luther nor Calvin included it in their doctrines. Speaking in tongues was frequently, it seems, an expression of tension. For example, a violent controversy between two Catholic factions, the Jesuits and the Jansenists, lasted nearly 80 years and produced glossolalists among

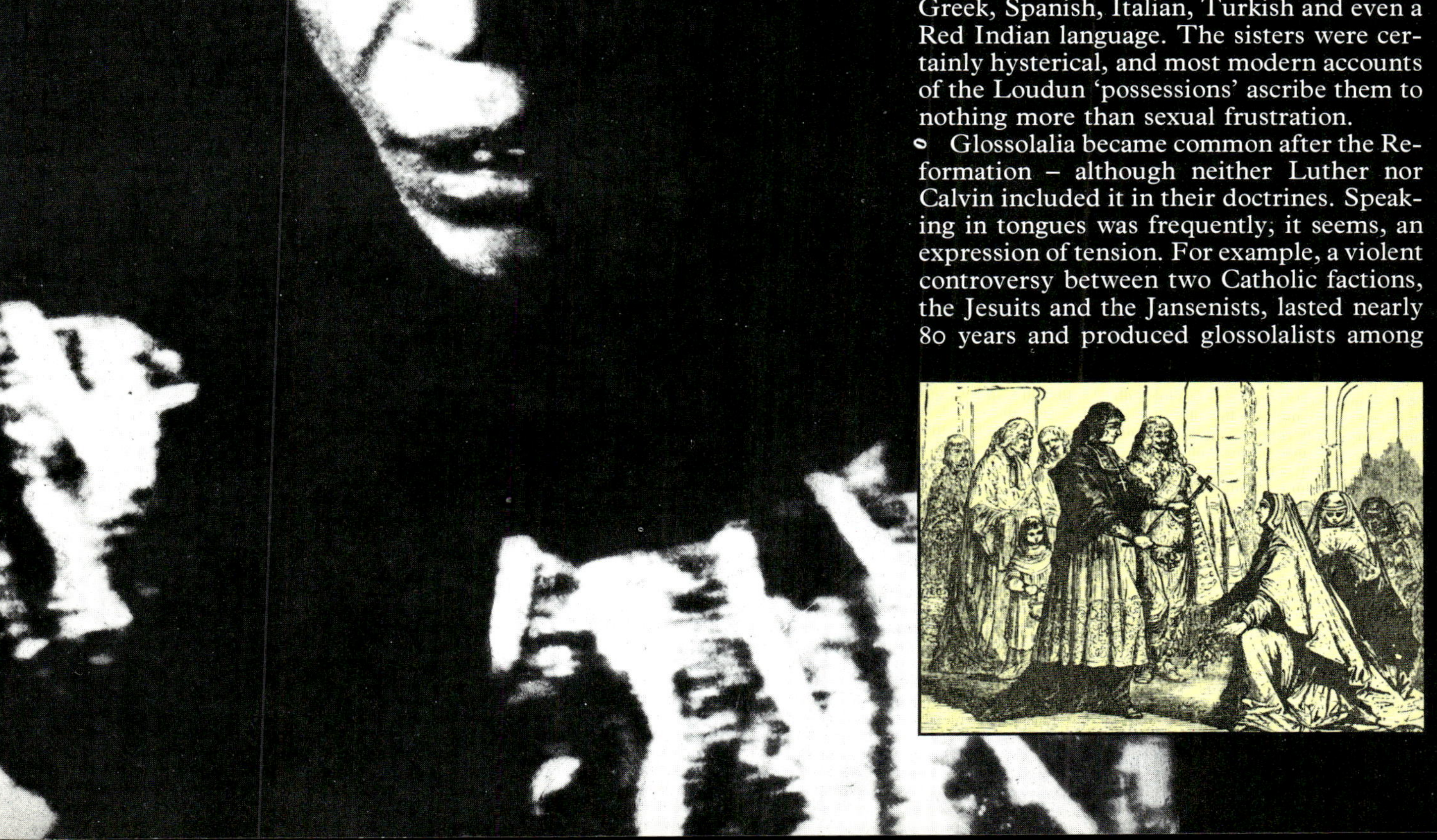

the latter. Coincidentally, extraordinary incidents occurred at that period among the Camisards, southern French Protestants living in the Cévennes mountains. When their freedom to worship was revoked in 1685 and attempts were made to force the Catholic faith on them, they rebelled. Three thousand of them resisted 60,000 royalist troops until they finally succumbed in 1705. The enormous strain on their guerilla communities, continuously harried and subjected to appalling atrocities when caught, resulted in supernormal happenings, including outbreaks of xenolalia. Thousands of 'little prophets of the Cévennes', children aged from 15 months upwards, preached lengthy sermons in excellent French, a language quite unlike their own dialect.

Some Camisards migrated to England. They had an influence on English 'enthusiasts', as Charismatic Christians were then called. Two generations later Ann Lee, converted to the United Society of Believers in Christ's Second Appearing ('the Shakers'), spoke in tongues and, examined by four erudite Anglican clergymen, addressed them in several apparently recognisable languages. Doubtless daunted by such learning, they advised she be left alone; but persecution drove her to America, where she founded the first Shaker settlement.

Recorded specimens of Shaker tongues, such as the following, are unimpressive. 'O calivin Christe I no vole/ Calivin Christe leste um/ I no vole vinim ne viste/ I no vole viste vum.' Nor did the Mormons (the Church of Jesus Christ of Latter-day Saints) produce anything better, even though their founder, Joseph Smith (1805–1844), was himself a glossolalist, and their articles of faith stated: 'We believe in the gifts of tongues . . . [and] the interpretation of tongues.' A sample is: 'Ah, man, oh, son of man,

Above: Shaker ritual dances often resulted in outbursts of tongues-speaking, which the Shakers regarded as a sign of grace. The gift of tongues is also accepted by the Mormon Church, founded by Joseph Smith (below)

ak ne commene en halle gaste en esak milkea, Jeremiah, Ezekiel, Nephi, Lehi, St John.' And there is the example of the dissertation on hunting that was produced by a speaker in the language of the Choctaw Indians. It was immediately interpreted as a florid account of the glories resulting from the completion of the Salt Lake City Temple. Modern Mormons recognise tongues as a real phenomenon, but of limited spiritual value, and understandably discourage them.

From 1830 onwards, not a year passed when someone did not speak in tongues somewhere in the Christian church. In Scandinavia in the 1840s there were outbursts of 'sermon-sickness' – hysterical 'enthusiasm' during worship – that included glossolalia. In the 1850s a great revival in the Russian Orthodox Church spilled over into Armenia, resulting in tongues-speaking there until the 1900s. In the later decades of the 19th century there were outbursts of glossolalia in Charismatic movements as far apart as North Carolina and Estonia, and in the evangelical campaigns conducted in England by Dwight L. Moody and Ira Sankey.

A sign of the Spirit

The worldwide vogue for speaking in tongues influenced the students of Bethel Bible College at Topeka, Kansas. Forty of them decided unanimously that 'something missing' in their Christian experience was Holy Ghost Baptism, of which the sign was speaking in tongues. On 31 December 1900 their minister, C. F. Parham, laid hands on a student, who broke into a stream of unintelligible syllables. Thirty others followed her example in succeeding days. This marked the beginning of modern Pentecostalism. In time, missions led by Parham took fire, resulting in hundreds of conversions, healings and glossolalic outbursts.

Some of the Pentecostalist movement's activities between the World Wars became famous – or notorious. In America Aimée

Messages from Mars

One of the strangest cases of written glossolalia involved the Swiss medium 'Hélène Smith' (a pseudonym for Catherine Élise Müller, 1861–1929). She claimed to leave her body and visit beings on the planet Mars who taught her the Martian language, which she both spoke and wrote (left).

Professor Theodore Flournoy of Geneva University investigated her – including her entranced speaking of Hindustani, a language unknown to her conscious self, and her 'Martian'. The Hindustani proved to be authentic but the 'Martian' had a syntax almost totally similar to her native French. Its untraceable vocabulary he dismissed as the product of her unusually brilliant, creative subconscious mind. And we now know that there are no signs of any life on Mars, let alone anyone writing or speaking Hélène Smith's 'Martian'.

Semple McPherson's International Church of the Foursquare Gospel was founded in 1921, with headquarters at its Hollywood temple. It rivalled the film capital itself in the glamour of its gospel presentation and the beauty of its choir of 'angels'. In England, George Jeffreys filled the Albert Hall every Easter from 1926 to 1939 with members of the Elim Foursquare Gospel. Today the largest of the Pentecostalist communions, the Assemblies of God, have congregations in almost every country where Christians are to be found. Although the emphasis on speaking in tongues has lessened, every Pentecostalist in the world – and they total some 20 million – believes that it exists and is a sign of the Holy Spirit's presence.

Speaking in tongues continued to occur in other Christian contexts, of course. It was one of the phenomena produced by a famous Christian sensitive, Teresa Neumann, who

Xenolalists of the 20th century: Rosemary (above), an English medium, often spoke in ancient Egyptian during seances; Teresa Neumann (right) allegedly cried out in Aramaic as she re-enacted Christ's passion

spent her life in Bavaria. On Good Friday 1926 stigmata appeared on her body and she appeared to live through Christ's passion, uttering Aramaic words and phrases, including some of those reportedly spoken by Jesus on the cross. Some observers believed she was in communication with a contemporary witness of Christ's crucifixion.

This feature – supposed communication with a person long dead – provides a link with Spiritualism. As Spiritualism developed during the last century, episodes frequently occurred of sensitives speaking in tongues. Some mediums claimed that spirits spoke through them in languages unknown to the mediums themselves and to all the sitters, except those for whom the messages were intended. Sometimes nobody present understood what was said until a linguist was called in to identify the tongue. Other mediums were 'direct-voice' specialists: spirit utterances emanated from the air around them, even while the mediums were conversing with their sitters. Some sensitives were

Above: Aimée Semple McPherson on stage at the Angelus Temple, Los Angeles, headquarters of the International Church of the Foursquare Gospel. Her dramatic sermons – accompanied by pageants, lantern slides, circuses and 'miraculous' healing sessions – became renowned throughout the United States

clairaudient: they 'heard' voices, often speaking in languages that they did not understand, and they would repeat the utterances as best they could.

A typical case was an English sensitive known only as Rosemary, who in the 1930s developed memories of former incarnations, of which the most important was in ancient Egypt. An Egyptologist, Howard Hulme, was among those who investigated her. Rosemary developed clairaudience of Egyptian words, and later Nona, the spirit of an Egyptian known to her in her former life, spoke through her. Gramophone recordings were made of some of her sessions. Once, for nearly two hours, Nona answered Hulme's prepared questions, using what were apparently the guttural aspirations, peculiar consonants and distinctive constructions of a language that died 3000 years ago. No living scholar, unfortunately, knows how the ancient Egyptian language was pronounced, and Rosemary's utterances, submitted to a selection of experts, drew an ambiguous verdict from them.

Despite the attention that 'tongues-speaking' has attracted over hundreds of years, its interpretation remains open. Is it the product of subconscious levels of the mind? Is a saint speaking 'with the tongues of angels' displaying a capacity to invent that we all possess? Is a medium speaking a language supposedly unknown to him in fact recollecting words seen and heard during his life and instantly forgotten at the conscious level? Or is xenolalia the result of 'reading' the minds of native speakers of the language being produced?

Modern research has cast little light on these conjectures. It has still less to say about the traditional suppositions that speakers in tongues are directly inspired by God or are taken over by the spirits of the dead. As always, such explanations demand faith – and will not be readily given up by those who have that faith.

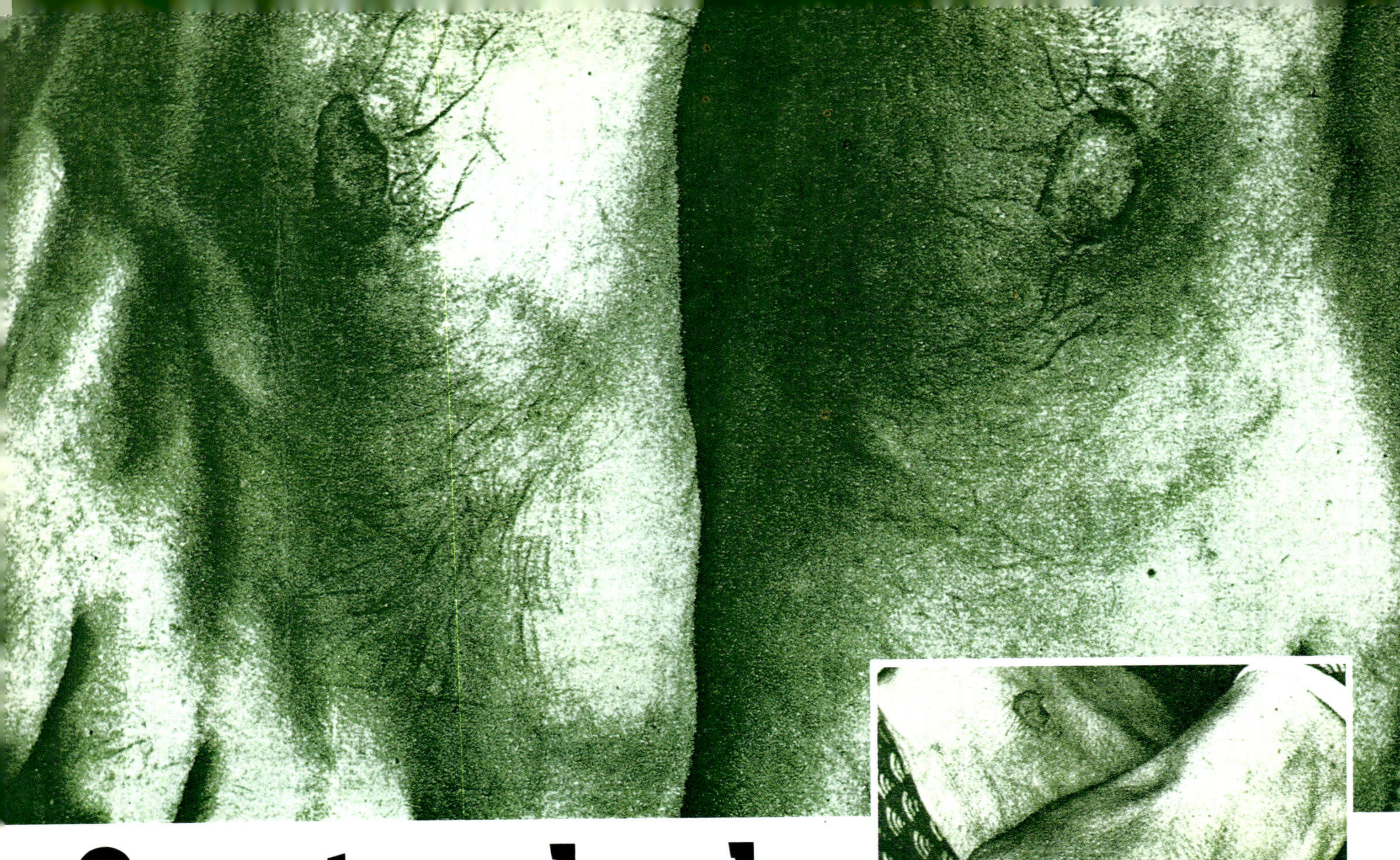

An outward and visible sign

Some deeply religious Christians share in Christ's sufferings in a bizarre and very literal way: their bodies develop wounds as if they had been crucified. BOB RICKARD examines the phenomenon of stigmata

ONE FRIDAY IN MARCH 1901 a young Italian girl prayed before a large lurid crucifix, and experienced a vision that changed her life. Her name was Gemma Galgani; she was 23 years old and an orphan. She wanted to become a Passionist nun, but was refused because of her spinal tuberculosis; instead, this simple, quiet and fervently devout girl became a domestic help in the local village. But her vision lifted her out of the ordinary, as she identified with Jesus's suffering, experiencing with combined agony and ecstasy each blow of the lash.

When she was found in her room by her adopted mother, her arms and back were covered with wounds like whip marks and her clothes were soaked in blood. From that day until she died two years later these stigmata appeared with astonishing regularity each Thursday, vanishing the next day. Her biographer, Father Germano di Stanislao, described how her wounds developed at the onset of her ecstasy, reddening slowly on the backs and palms of both hands;

Above and above right: these details from a 1949 photograph show the stigmatised feet and hands of Arthur Otto Moock, the 'Hamburg stigmatic' whose wounds appeared on 13 December 1943. His flesh was pierced as if by large nails, and fresh blood issued from the holes. Sceptics who are presented with stigmata tend to fall back on accusations of fraud (meaning that the wounds are self-inflicted), but in almost all known cases of stigmata there is no evidence to support this theory

'. . . under the epidermis a rent in the flesh was seen to open by degrees . . . after a little the membrane burst and on those innocent hands were seen the marks of flesh wounds.' They were very deep, apparently passing right through the hand itself. They were full of blood, 'partly flowing, partly congealed', and out of consideration for the pain they caused the girl, Father Germano never probed them. On Friday the wounds closed quickly, leaving only a whitish mark by Sunday. The location of the marks varied from week to week, said Father Germano, sometimes appearing on the hands or feet only, sometimes bleeding through an unruptured skin. At other times the appearance of nails with thick heads could be seen in the wounds, formed out of mounds and ridges of darkened flesh and dark, solidified blood.

Despite the scorn of sceptics, there can be no doubt about the reality of stigmatic phenomena. They have occurred too many times under close medical scrutiny to be a fiction. And although the greatest body of evidence lies in the hands of the Catholic Church and is inaccessible, we have more than enough proof of their existence from the testimony of doctors and other impeccable witnesses cited in many official biographies, and in modern times the marks have been photographically recorded.

So what are these marks? Popularly the word *stigmata* is taken to mean the wounds suffered by Christ during his arrest, trial and execution – events known collectively as the Passion – and which are reproduced on the body of the stigmatic. Traditionally these are the wounds corresponding to those made by the nails in the hands and feet, and the spear wound in the side of the chest. There are also supplemental stigmata, often appearing on their own: scourge marks on the body, holes in the forehead as if made by a crown of thorns, a deformed shoulder said to be from the weight of the cross, and more bizarrely, curious symbols were said to be imprinted onto the heart and other internal organs.

Genuine stigmata have very interesting physiological characteristics that differentiate them from ordinary flesh wounds. The blood that flows from them is clean arterial blood with no trace of disease. The wounds may stay open for long periods, sometimes years, with a complete inhibition of normal healing processes, despite which they remain free of infection and inflammation. In a fashion that is not understood, these wounds can come and go spontaneously, but are usually associated with a special state of consciousness, related to trance, in which the stigmatic experiences a union with the suffering of Christ's Passion, and which provides the 'pattern' for what is happening to the stigmatic's own body. Unlike any other kind of wounds (except perhaps some of more obvious psychosomatic origin), most stigmata recur regularly, some during Lent and Easter every year, and some on special Church feast days only, and others every Friday, especially Easter Friday.

The first stigmatic

Although St Paul wrote '. . . let no man trouble me, for I bear in my body the marks of the Lord Jesus' (Galatians 6:17), we have no definite evidence of stigmata until 1224, the year in which St Francis of Assisi was stigmatised while in a spiritual retreat on Mount Alvernia, in the Italian Apennines. Praying outside his cave, he saw a winged seraph in the skies, then fell in a swoon. Contemporary accounts say the stigmata appeared as the saint struggled up from the ground and called for help.

His biographer, Thomas Celano, writing three years after the saint's death in 1226, described these unique wounds:

> His hands and feet seemed pierced in the midst by nails, the heads of the nails appearing in the inner part of the hands and in the upper part of the feet, and their points over against them. . . . Moreover his right side, as if it had been pierced by a lance, was overlaid with a scar, and often shed forth blood so that his tunic and drawers were . . . sprinkled with sacred blood.

It is interesting to note that Celano is describing not just a wound but a nail-like formation of tissue apparently lodged in the wound. Those in the feet protruded so much that St Francis could not walk. At the saint's death many filed past his body, which was still displaying these peculiar formations 'marvellously wrought by the power of God . . . implanted in the flesh in such wise that if they were pressed in on either side they straightway, as if they were one piece of sinew, projected on the other.' So bizarre is this detail that many historians have dismissed it as an embellishment, but medical testimony to similar formations – for example those in the hands of St Gemma Galgani – suggest its authenticity.

This dramatic event obviously made a deep and lasting impression on the medieval imagination. Soon other cases were reported – genuine and spontaneous stigmatisations that were thoroughly witnessed and documented. And they have been occurring right

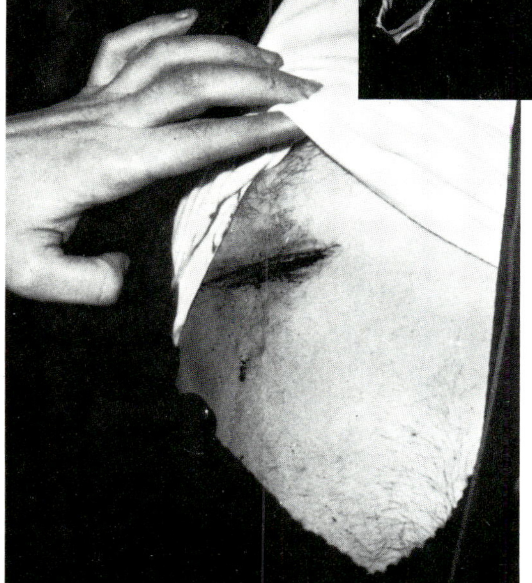

Clemente Dominguez, a Spanish mystic and self-appointed 'Pope', regularly developed stigmata such as the 'crown of thorns' (right) and the side-wound (below) during his trances in the 1970s. He was no humble or modest stigmatic; instead of retiring from the public gaze he flaunted his wounds and revelled in the adoration accorded him by those who believed him to be a saint

observation and pursuit, not to mention the dispassionate scrutiny of the Vatican.

The life of St Mary Magdalen de'Pazzi, a revered Carmelite mystic, was one of torment, yet in a close examination of her case one tends to agree with Dr Eric Dingwall, whose researches led him to believe that she was a 'classic example of the ascetic female flagellant and masochistic exhibitionist with a sadistic streak.' In between her raptures were intervals in which she keenly felt the 'temptations' of her body and would resort to rolling in thorn bushes or whipping herself with nettles for distraction. She soon believed she was being attacked – even sexually assaulted – and would swipe at the air about her, throw stones at her invisible assailants, or convulse on the ground reacting to unseen blows. Naturally the Devil was blamed, obviously being outraged by her sanctity. St Mary's initiating vision came in 1585, in which, it is said, St Augustine wrote upon her heart, in crimson letters, *Verbum caro factum est* ('The Word was made Flesh');

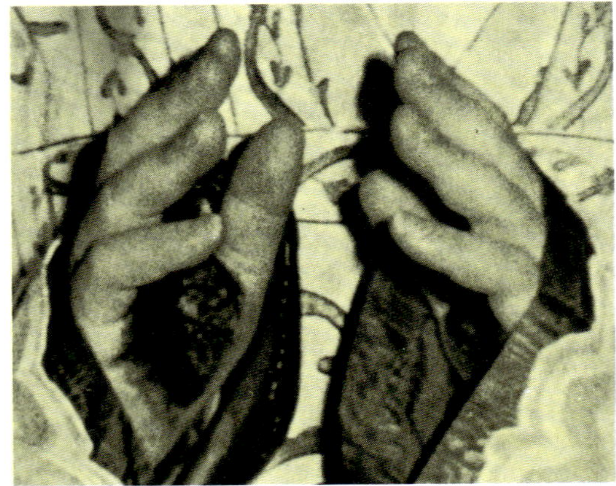

eight days later, in another rapture, Christ offered her his crown of thorns, and she exchanged hearts with him. Thereafter her stigmata were in perpetual evidence and she was constantly fainting with pain or swooning in ecstasy. Most stigmatics have similar visions in which Christ himself invites them to share his suffering.

The variety among stigmata deserves a study in itself. St Catherine of Ricci (who died in 1590), St Gemma Galgani and others sometimes had deformed shoulders, and complained of the pain and great weight of an invisible cross. In the 13th century Helena Brumsin bore savage scourge marks, as did Anne Catherine Emmerich nearly 600 years later. Archangela Tardera similarly suffered during a vision in 1608, which left her blind several years before her death, and her stigmata and the scourge marks were still visible on her undecayed body many years later (see page 31). St Catherine of Siena bore her stigmata invisibly, though she felt the pain for five years until her death in 1380, when they finally became visible. The wounds could still be seen when her incorrupted corpse was 'translated' and different parts of

up to the present; indeed, they may even be more frequent today than ever before. An extensive listing of stigmatics was attempted in 1894 by Dr Imbert-Gourbeyre, who reached the total of 321 cases. A survey conducted in the 1950s by the subject's great authority, Father Herbert Thurston, suggests that this figure is conservative.

Another curious statistic is the extraordinarily high proportion of female stigmatics; in Dr Imbert-Gourbeyre's figures only 41 were male, and only one of these was stigmatised fully – St Francis himself. Other male stigmatics are mentioned by Father Thurston and also by the occult writer Montague Summers, but they are without the full complement of marks, do not suffer periodic bleeding, or lack proper authentification.

The only other known fully stigmatised man since St Francis has been the Capuchin friar Padre Pio Forgione, most of whose humble life was spent at the monastery of San Giovanni Rotondo at Foggia, Italy, and who died in 1968. In 1915, aged 28, he emerged from a long meditation with a stinging sensation in his hands. Three years later he was alone in the choir, celebrating the Feast of the Stigmata of St Francis, when his piercing cry brought his brothers running. They found him unconscious, bleeding profusely from the traditional sites of all five of Christ's wounds. He begged for this to be kept a secret, but word spread. Regularly, as he lifted the Host during mass, he would pass into ecstasy and a cupful of blood and serum would flow from his wounds every day. He could move only with pain and difficulty but tried to remain private and to conceal his hands; however, public adulation was so great that he was under almost constant

Padre Pio Forgione, who died in 1968, was one of the most revered and best-known of all stigmatics. Since he was stigmatised in 1915 at the age of 28, this Capuchin friar sought to hide his terrible hand-wounds (right), appearing in public only to say mass (above). There is no doubt that his stigmata were real; doctors examined them many times over the years and discovered his palms to be permanently pierced right through. Padre Pio suffered constant pain in his hands but bore it uncomplainingly her were sent all over Europe as relics. The wounds of St Mary Francis of the Five Wounds (who died in 1791) completely perforated her hands, and her confessor more than once poked his finger right through them. And like several other stigmatics Magdalena de la Cruz, who was stigmatised for 39 years until her death in 1560, was also seen levitating.

Perhaps the most famous female stigmatic of the 20th century is Teresa Neumann. Like St Gemma, she came from a poor background and took up menial work until mysterious illnesses incapacitated her. In 1926, when she was 28, her afflictions were spontaneously cured after a vision that left her stigmatised. For 32 years she gushed blood from hands, feet, side and forehead during most Fridays – sometimes losing as much as a pint (0.5 litre) of blood and 8 pounds (3.6 kilograms) in weight. Yet she was back to normal by Sunday. For most of this time she was under medical supervision, in the Bavarian village of Konnersreuth, and was also watched closely by the Bishop of Ratisbon. Doctors examined her thoroughly – taking advantage of her trances and periods of unconsciousness – and frequently described the appearance of wounds with the nail-like formations first seen in St Francis of Assisi. One observer noted that, as the years went by, wounds that had been on the backs of her hands developed instead in the palms.

According to Johannes Steiner's biography of Teresa Neumann, which was published in 1967, and which includes photographs of her unique rectangular hand wounds, no food or liquid – except the Communion wafer and wine – passed her lips for the last 35 years of her life, and many

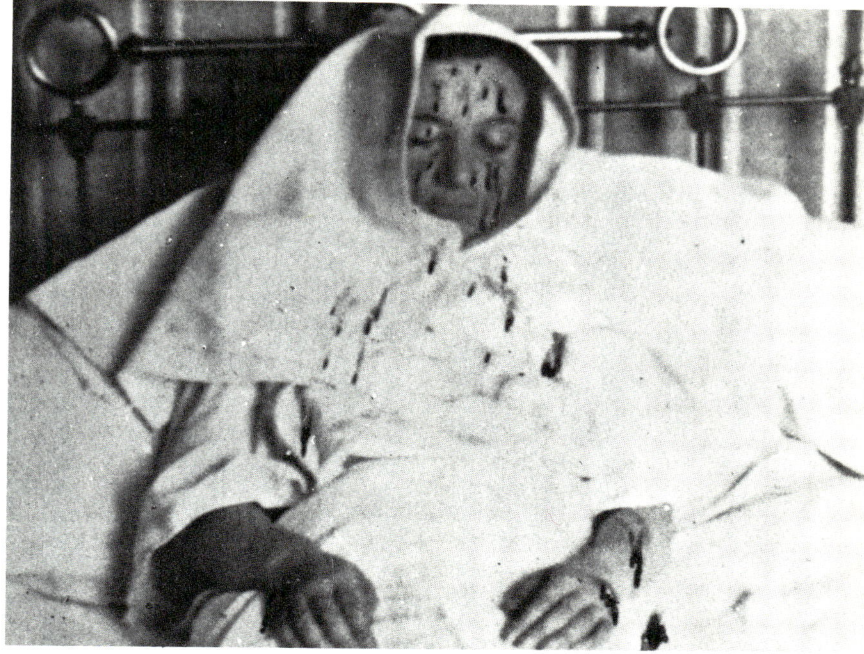

Above: Teresa Neumann, the poor Bavarian whose mysterious illnesses were banished when she was stigmatised in 1926. Every Friday until her death in 1962 she suffered Christ's Passion; wounds appeared in her hands, sides and forehead. She lost weight yet she was always back to normal every Sunday. She also spoke in Aramaic during trances and is said to have taken no food for 35 years

Left: St Francis of Assisi was stigmatised immediately after his vision of a winged seraph. The first recorded stigmatic, this 13th-century saint exhibited nail-like formations – apparently made of toughened sinew – protruding from the wounds in his feet

experiments by different doctors confirmed this astonishing fact. Moreover, her excreta ceased after 1930 and her intestinal tract simply withered – yet despite this she remained fairly active, having ecstasies and visions right up to her death in 1962.

Cases of stigmata continue to be reported. Of the many that could be mentioned, two are of special interest. The first is that of little Cloretta Robertson, who was 10 when she was stigmatised for 19 days over Easter in 1972. She was studied by two psychiatrists, who reported in *General Psychiatry* (May 1974) that they had seen drops of blood oozing through a discoloured patch of skin on her palms when they put her hands under a microscope. Although her marks did not return, this case is especially remarkable, because not only is Cloretta a normal American girl – she is no brooding mystic – she is also the first known black and non-Catholic stigmatic.

The other case is that of Teresa Musco, who died in 1976. As reported in *National Enquirer* of 11 January 1977, she was a poor Italian seamstress who accurately predicted she would die, aged 33 – the same age as Christ. She was stigmatised in a vision in 1969, and though normally illiterate and poorly educated, in her trances she would both speak and write Aramaic (the Semitic language spoken by Christ and the Apostles). Her hands were completely pierced. In her presence, a statue was once seen to weep blood (see pages 9–13), and her corpse (although it was later to decay) was free of rigor mortis for nearly a week after her death. Inevitably a movement has started to petition the Vatican to make this simple and devout woman a saint.

Who are the stigmatics?

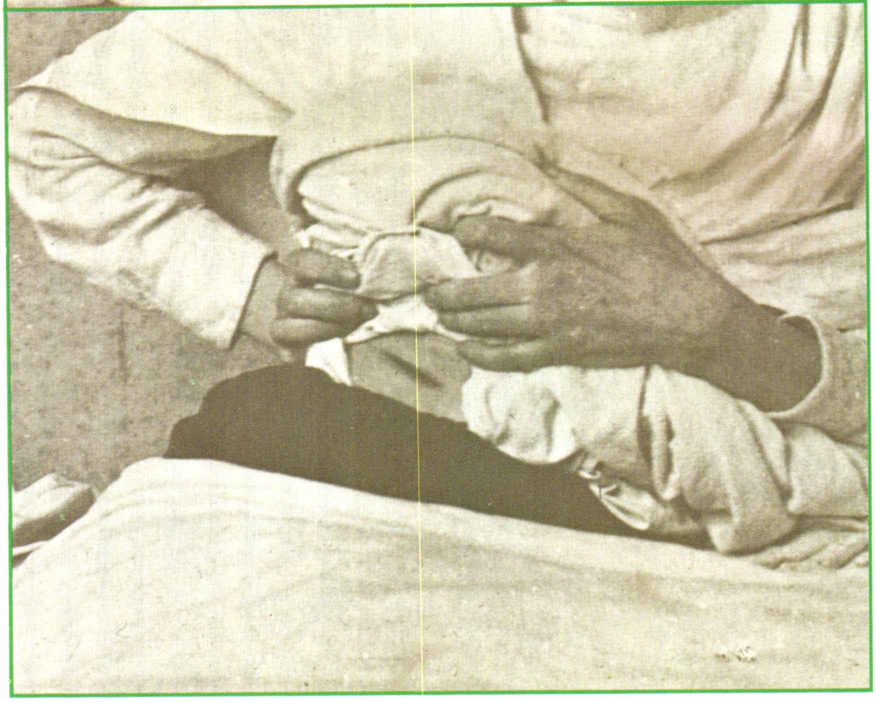

What causes the physical phenomenon of stigmata? Is it, as many Christians believe, the result of meditation on Christ's sufferings by a saintly person? Or are the marks of psychosomatic origin, visible evidence of a form of hysteria?

THE CURIOUS PHENOMENON of stigmata – the mysterious appearance of wounds resembling, as far as one can tell, those suffered by Christ during his Passion – is almost exclusively found among members of the Roman Catholic Church. Its records, therefore, contain the essential information for a researcher in this field. Yet the Church cannot be said to be objective about the phenomenon, for it allows for 'divine' and 'diabolical' stigmata, depending in theory on the saintliness or otherwise of the individual stigmatic. Although in practice the dividing line may frequently have been drawn for political reasons, one criterion was consistently applied: stigmatics who exploited their wounds for fame or wealth were demonstrably 'diabolical'.

If ostentatious display is a factor in determining the 'divine' or 'diabolical' origin of stigmata, then the case of Elizabeth of Herkenrode should have been damned long ago. This 13th-century nun spent most of her life in almost continual trance, enacting the whole of the Passion each 24 hours, often portraying Christ and several of his tormentors by turns. Father Thurston, the Roman

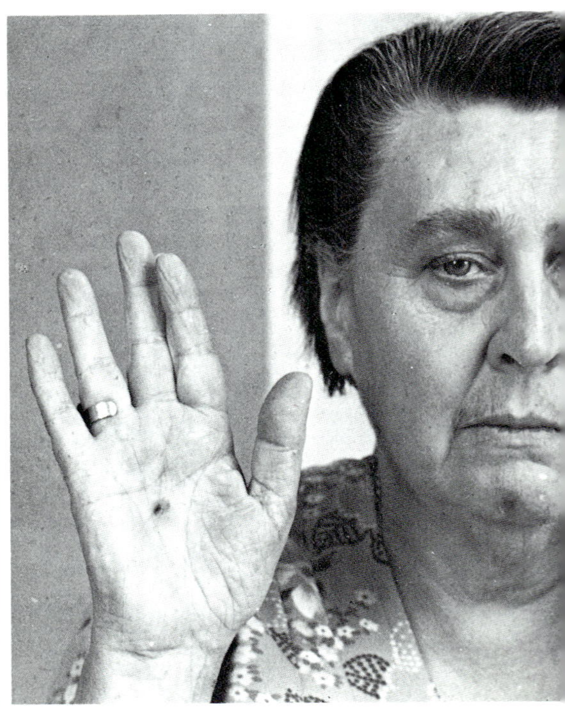

Catholic historian, describes a scene, drawing on contemporary accounts:

Catching hold of the bosom of her own dress with her right hand she would pull herself to the right and then with the left hand she would drag herself in the opposite direction. At another time, stretching out her arm and raising her fist threateningly, she would strike herself a violent blow on the jaw so that her whole body seemed to reel and totter under the impact.

She was, apparently, dramatising scenes and actions experienced in her visions, and at the appropriate moments the scourge marks, those of the 'crown of thorns', and the stigmata would open up on her body and gush blood.

Similarly, Domenica Lazarri (who died in 1848) and the English stigmatic Teresa Higginson (whose 'blessed death' came 50 years later) beat themselves mercilessly with their fists – Domenica's self-inflicted blows were so loud that they were heard out on the street, and Teresa believed firmly that her beatings were administered by the Devil himself. The revered mystic and stigmatic St Mary Magdalen de'Pazzi was undoubtedly motivated by the ecstatic union with God that inspired her writings. but the relish with which she exhorted her superiors to flog her and with which she whipped her novices is hardly edifying. One can sympathise with Father Thurston's perplexity as he wrote:

There are many instances of stigmatisation where imposture is out of the question but in which many of the details recorded are suggestive rather of disease than of that showing forth of the divine attributes which we associate with the idea of a miracle.

On the other hand, there are the sceptical scientists who, without investigation, prefer to dismiss these stories and their frequently unimpeachable witnesses as subject to hoax, delusion and wishful thinking.

However, there are many who believe that the 'stigmatic complex' corresponds to certain psychoneurotic conditions, particularly that known as 'hysteria'. The major problem here arises over the popular misunderstanding of the meaning of the word. To most people – including most Catholic theologians – it conjures up an image of highly excitable neuropaths; weak-minded, pathological liars, who are given to tantrums and excessive scenes in order to get their own way. Call someone hysterical and almost inevitably it is taken as an insult.

The clinical meaning of the term is, however, quite different. Before the 20th century hysteria was believed to be exclusively a woman's complaint – the very word is Greek for 'wandering womb'. But psychiatrists dealing with the effects of extreme stress on soldiers in the trenches discovered that men can suffer from 'hysterical' symptoms too. It became clear that there is a hysterical *personality* and there are hysterical *symptoms* (which may or may not go together in the same person).

Uses of hysteria

It is the hysterical *personality* that indulges in the dramatic and exaggerated behaviour commonly associated with 'hysteria' but the *symptoms* can afflict anyone in circumstances of stress, heightened emotion or inner conflict. They may even be useful to us when we are in danger. There are many cases on record of soldiers in action who are suddenly smitten with inexplicable paralysis or blindness. Tests show that they are not malingering – the symptoms are 'real' – but the cause is discovered to be hysterical. The soldier cannot face the battle any longer but because of his training and fear of being labelled a coward he cannot give in to his fear and run away. Instead his brain resolves the conflict for him, causing his body to cease functioning as a fighting force.

There are also cases where the symptoms are revealed – under hypnosis, for example – to be literal translations of everyday sayings. 'I can't go on' has been 'translated' by the brain into hysterical lameness, 'I can't face it' into blindness, and even 'it's all a pain in the neck' into the matching physical symptom. So certain allegedly holy manifestations such as the appearance of a wedding-ring-like ridge or indentation around the appropriate finger of a nun (or 'bride of Christ') may also be seen as a form of hysteria.

Hysterical symptoms are, psychiatrists agree, not incompatible with ordinary lives nor with those of the highest sanctity. Hysteria does not 'explain away' stigmata, as

Far left: Teresa Neumann, stigmatised during Holy Week in 1926, shows the wounds in his hands and in his side

Right: 'Mortado', the music hall performer who was billed as 'the only man with marks of crucifixion'. The origin of his stigmata is obscure, but his ostentatious display of them left Roman Catholics in no doubt: he was quite simply a puppet of the Devil

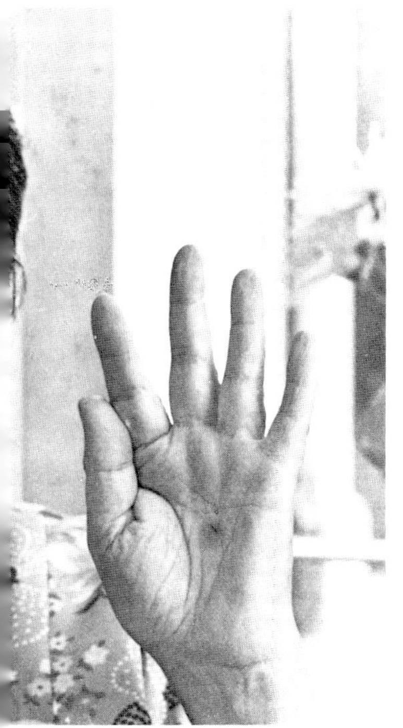

Below: the English stigmatic Ethel Chapman, who died in the late 1970s, shows her hand-wounds. Every Easter for many years she felt as if nails were being driven into her palms and red holes appeared

many Church apologists fear, but it could well describe the mechanism of this bizarre phenomena.

Yet most Roman Catholics still regard a 'hysterical' explanation of stigmata as an insult and a blasphemy. They point out that stigmatics such as St Gemma Galgani, Padre Pio or St Teresa of Avila were humble, quiet and downright unexcitable, therefore obviously not 'hysterical'. But a closer look at the lives of these 'quiet' stigmatics reveals a history of mysterious maladies and an abnormal physical sensitivity. They were subject to a range of inexplicable illnesses including blackouts, fits, paralysis, blindness and so on. Many were victims of tuberculosis, which heightens suggestibility. And, interestingly, the visions that stigmatised them also marked the end of their many mystery illnesses.

Signs of a shaman?

Many stigmatics develop the sort of behaviour associated with the shaman (or witch doctor) of more primitive societies: going into trances, having visions, exhibiting the ability to heal, levitate, prophesy or be immune to fire. Many of them also revealed multiple personalities – among these were Teresa Higginson, Constante Mary Castreca (a 17th-century Italian nun), Mother Beatrice Mary of Jesus and Teresa Neumann – who also spoke in tongues (see page 75). It may be that stigmatics are the Catholic Church's equivalent of shamans, but even so, multiple personality is now recognised as a hysterical symptom and it may be that many of their other 'gifts', including the stigmata, have the same base.

Another clue to the hysterical foundation of stigmata comes from the component of suggestibility. The wounds of St Veronica Giuliani (who died in 1727) opened and bled at the command of her confessor, just as the Belgian stigmatic Louise Lateau and others could be recalled instantly from their highest ecstasies by the command of their superiors. The side-wound of Anne Catherine Emmerich was known to resemble the unusual Y-shaped crucifix in the church at Coesfeld in Germany where she meditated as a child. And the scourge marks of St Gemma Galgani apparently reproduced exactly those on her favourite crucifix.

This subjective element in the patterning of stigmata, and the great variety of forms it takes, would also seem to argue for a hysterical foundation. The wounds have been known to range from simple red spots to cross-shaped fissures, to round, oblong or square holes in the hands; 'nail-heads' have been on the backs of hands or in the palms and on either right or left foot, even in the soles, and the side-wounds have shown similar variations in right or left sides, according to how the stigmatic imagines Christ was crucified. Perhaps significantly, there are no known examples of wounds occurring in the

Above: Louise Lateau, the Belgian who claimed to have been stigmatised during a vision in January 1868, when she was 18. Her wounds remained visible for 15 years until her death. She was exhaustively – and often painfully – tested by many doctors during that time but her wounds remained genuinely 'miraculous'

Right: weeping blood, a rare phenomenon closely related to true stigmata and equally mysterious

wrists, the site of the wounds suggested by researchers into the Turin Shroud (see page 42). But now that this is quite common knowledge among the devout, future stigmatics could well exhibit wrist wounds.

There have been many attempts to reproduce stigmata by hypnosis but the only results have been a short-lived reddening of the skin, or sporadic bleeding. This pales in comparison to the dramatic piercings and copious bleedings of genuine stigmata, which have defied normal healing processes and stayed with the stigmatics for most of their lives. Yet it cannot be overlooked that there is a high correlation between the histories and phenomena of stigmatics and those of clinical hysteria; the difference is merely one of context and degree. Outside the religious context, where there is no 'need' for stigmata to take the form stylised by the

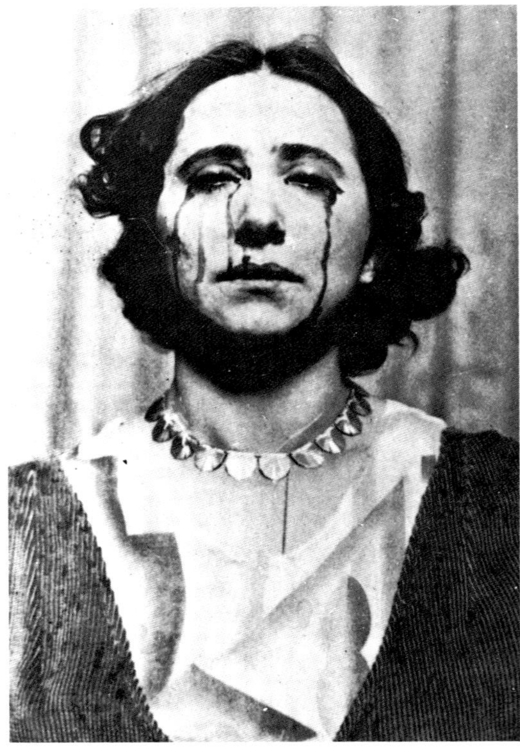

crucifixion of Christ, there are many kinds of paranormal and even psychological phenomena where spontaneous formations or lesions of the skin may develop. One such case was that of Eleonore Zugun, a famous poltergeist victim, studied by Harry Price in the 1920s, whose skin showed weals, bite marks and even raised lettering when she believed she was being attacked by a devil only she could see.

In many, if not all, cases of stigmata the effects seem to stem somehow from the subconscious mind of the stigmatic. If we could begin to understand the process of cause and effect involved then perhaps many more strange phenomena would be understood. But in that case the miraculous would become the mundane and for many the loss would be hard to bear.

Christ's suffering and death are at the very centre of Christian belief. But what if he did not die on the cross, but married and had children – whose descendants are alive today? STAN GOOCH examines the evidence

THE DISCOVERY OF secret documents, and possibly a hoard of treasure, and perhaps, some have suggested, mummified relics of Christ, in the small village of Rennes-le-Château in south-west France, made a poor village priest into a millionaire (see page 14). But it also set in motion a chain of events that led to the discovery of a secret that, if it is true, is the most disturbing revelation in the history of Christianity.

The story of the clues that led them to their amazing conclusion is related by Michael Baigent, Richard Leigh and Henry Lincoln, in their bestseller *The holy blood and the Holy Grail*. The book has aroused the

The crucifixion, here depicted by Giotto (*c*.1266-1337), has been a source of inspiration for countless artists. But did Christ actually *die* on the cross? The authors of a powerfully argued book, *The holy blood and the Holy Grail* (1982), believe he did not – and put forward a completely new interpretation

extremes of either instant enthusiasm or instant antagonism in its readers. Establishment critics, fairly predictably, have tended to dismiss the book as a wild romance based on the flimsiest evidence. Nevertheless, such comment is both unfair and demonstrably untrue. No one can simply sweep aside the mass of evidence assembled by the authors, and their presentation of it is admirably cautious. This series of chapters, far from describing the authors of *The holy blood and the Holy Grail* as incautious, will show that they have seriously *under*estimated the extent and implications of the material they have gathered, and that there is much more they have overlooked. A still greater mystery lies behind the secrets that they document.

The authors of *The holy blood and the Holy Grail* present evidence of a powerful and ancient international mystery, and of a many layered secret society whose widespread

The royal house of Jesus

Left: Richard Leigh, Henry Lincoln and Michael Baigent (left to right), authors of *The holy blood and the Holy Grail*, in which they put forward the startling theory that a secret society, the Priory of Sion, guards the interests of the blood descendants of Christ. They claim these descendants are ready, when the occasion arises, to assume a leading role in the government of Europe – and perhaps the world

influence extends right to the present. The starting point of the authors' investigation of the mystery concerned a massive buried treasure; their final conclusion is an astonishing claim that Jesus Christ married Mary Magdalene and produced children. Descendants of these children, they believe, intermarried with other kings and rulers of ancient times, notably with the Merovingians, the first dynasty of Frankish kings in Gaul; and direct descendants of these are alive and well, awaiting the call – or opportunity – to assume a leading role in the politics of Europe, and possibly of the world. That, at least, is where the authors' evidence leads them.

The connection between the holy blood and the Holy Grail of the title of Baigent, Leigh and Lincoln's book is made through an ingenious wordplay. The Holy Grail is a complex and mysterious concept. For some authors it is a stone, for others a repository for saintly relics. But most often it is the cup used by Jesus at the Last Supper, in which his blood was caught as he hung upon the cross. In many of the early Grail manuscripts, it is referred to as the Sangraal; and even in the later version by Malory, it is the Sangreal. Baigent, Leigh and Lincoln argue that some such form – Sangraal or Sangreal – must have been close to the original. And, dividing this into two words in a way that seems entirely reasonable, they conclude that the word may not originally have been 'San Graal' or 'San Greal' – from which the English translation 'Holy Grail' comes – but 'Sang Raal' or 'Sang Réal'. 'Or,' as they triumphantly conclude, 'to employ the modern spelling, Sang Royal. Royal blood.' That is, the legend of the transportation of the Holy Grail from Judea to Europe is not the legend of the bringing of an artefact – but

Right: a Knight Templar. The authors of *The holy blood and the Holy Grail* argue that the Knights Templar, an immensely powerful order of warrior monks that flourished from 1124 to 1307, were only the military arm of a yet more powerful organisation, the Priory of Sion – the guardians of the interests of Christ's descendants

the true history of the arrival of the descendants of Jesus and Mary Magdalene, carriers of the royal blood or 'Sang Réal', in France.

It is, to say the least, an impressive hypothesis. But the claim for the existence of these living descendants of Christ is a weak link in Baigent, Leigh and Lincoln's argument, a less than convincing interpretation of the evidence. It seems improbable, for instance, that in all the dozens and dozens of generations that have elapsed since the time of Christ one or other descendant would not have succumbed to the temptation to announce 'I am the lineal Son of Christ.' We find no whisper of any such announcement in

the whole of 2000 years; nor, indeed, any really solid evidence of any actual progeny. Instead we have a mass of evidence and stories referring obliquely to a central mystery, and to specifics like the precious Holy Grail, to talking skulls and severed heads, to blood as a substance and as a symbol, to alchemical wonders, and to some kind of guiding society of elders or initiates. Yet, even if Baigent, Leigh and Lincoln are correct in their belief in the survival of the descendants of Christ, the central mystery, on their own evidence, is something still wider and older. The Christ story and the events that surround it are but one piece (an important piece, certainly) of a still larger mosaic.

Warrior monks

Baigent, Leigh and Lincoln allege that the Knights Templar were among the major custodians of the secret. This band of warrior monks was formed around 1120 for the purpose of protecting pilgrims to the Holy Land. With astonishing rapidity, they became both a powerful military force and, effectively, the bankers of Europe (see page 20). Their ascendancy came to an abrupt end, however, on the night of Friday, 13 October 1307, when, on the orders of King Philippe IV, all the Templars in France were arrested. Trials and punishments followed, and the order was finally suppressed, by order of the Pope, in 1312.

The authors of *The holy blood and the Holy Grail* have uncovered documents that suggest that the Templars were the military wing of an older mystical alliance called the Priory of Sion – an alliance that, they claim, was created and continues to exist for the purpose of protecting and promoting the interests of the direct descendants of Christ. The list of the leaders of the Priory of Sion through the ages includes Leonardo da Vinci, Sandro Filipepi – better known as Botticelli – Isaac Newton, Victor Hugo and Claude Debussy, as well as a number of seemingly unimportant French aristocratic figures.

During the trials of the French Templars in 1308, one member of the order testified that on his induction he was shown a crucifix

---

Bride of Christ?

Was Jesus married? According to Michael Baigent, Richard Leigh and Henry Lincoln, in their book *The holy blood and the Holy Grail*, the gospels themselves suggest he was.

They cite, in particular, Jesus's first major miracle, the transmutation of water into wine at the wedding feast at Cana (John 2:1-13). According to the familiar story, Jesus and his mother, Mary, are invited – or 'called' – to a country wedding feast. For reasons not explained in the text of the gospel, Mary calls on Jesus to replenish the wine – something that would normally be the responsibility of the host, or bridegroom's family. Why should she do this – unless the wedding was, in fact, Jesus's own? More direct evidence comes immediately after the miracle has been performed when 'the governor of the feast called *the bridegroom*, and saith unto him, Every man at the beginning doth set forth good wine; and when men have well drunk, then that which is worse: but *thou* hast kept the good wine until now.' (Editorial italics.) The implication is clear: the wedding is Christ's own.

If this surmise is correct, the obvious question is: who was Christ's wife? Again, Baigent, Leigh and Lincoln have their answers ready. The two obvious candidates, from a reading of the synoptic gospels, are Mary Magdalene and Mary of Bethany. The authors contend that these two characters are actually one woman, and that she was indeed the wife of Christ.

Christ meets Mary Magdalene in the garden after his resurrection. Is this a meeting between husband and wife?

Additional support for this theory comes from some of the apocryphal gospels, suppressed early in the history of the Church. In the gospel of Mary, for example, Peter speaks to Mary Magdalene in these words: 'Sister, we know that the Saviour loved you more than the rest of women. Tell us the words of the Saviour which you remember – which you know but we do not.' Subsequently Peter complains to the other disciples, 'Did he really speak privately with a woman and not openly to us? Are we to turn about and all listen to her? Did he prefer her to us?' Later one of the other disciples consoles him: 'Surely the Saviour knows her very well. That is why he loved her more than us.'

The gospel of Philip is still more emphatic: 'And the companion of the Saviour is Mary Magdalene. But Christ loved her more than all the disciples and used to kiss her often on her mouth. The rest of the disciples were offended by it and expressed disapproval. They said to him, "Why do you love her more than all of us?" The Saviour answered and said to them, "Why do I not love you like her?"'

Towards the end of the same gospel, Baigent, Leigh and Lincoln point out, there is one more relevant passage – which, to those prepared to admit it as valid evidence, clinches the argument: 'There is the Son of man and there is the son of the Son of man. The Lord is the Son of man, and the son of the Son of man is he who is created through the Son of man.'

and told, 'Set not much faith in this, for it is too young.' Another was told, 'Christ is a false prophet,' and a third, 'Do not believe that the man Jesus whom the Jews crucified in Outremer [Palestine] is God and that he can save you.' Apart from specific charges, the Templars were accused in general of denying, trampling and spitting on the cross. In the light of this it is perhaps significant that, in his decorations of the church of Notre Dame de France in London, executed in 1960, Jean Cocteau, who allegedly succeeded Debussy as the leader of the Priory of Sion, depicts himself standing with his back to the cross. What is more, at the foot of the cross he paints a gigantic rose – an extremely ancient mystical symbol.

Baigent, Leigh and Lincoln admit that no satisfactory explanation has been advanced

A detail from an anonymous 15th-century painting of the Last Supper, from the monastery of St Neophytos in Cyprus. The mysterious object known as the Holy Grail is often identified as the cup used at the Last Supper – a vessel that was also used, so the legend goes, to catch Christ's blood as he hung upon the cross. But the authors of *The holy blood and the Holy Grail* argue that the legends surrounding the Holy Grail refer to something quite different – the holy bloodline, or family, of Christ

germinate'. This last charge may seem innocuous enough at first sight. But in fact it links Templar practice and tradition firmly with ancient and pre-Christian fertility religions, with that which was not 'too young' to have real occult powers. There is much else besides that Baigent, Leigh and Lincoln do not consider – for example, the fact that the Templars shouted 'Selah' and other 'meaningless' words when prostrating themselves before the heads. 'Selah' appears occasionally at the ends of verses of the Psalms, and it has been conjectured by scholars that it is a musical direction to choirmasters. But there is another possible explanation: could Selah be a corruption of Shiloh? Shiloh is an ancient site in the mountains near Jerusalem – and Jerusalem was where the Templars originated – that was regarded by the ancient Jews as a holy place and whose name was often used in the Old Testament to indicate the 'Messiah'. Nevertheless, like Jerusalem itself and the Jewish Sabbath, Shiloh was considered by the Jews to be a woman, something that may be highly significant.

Betrayal and downfall

The Knights Templar were betrayed to the Inquisition and all simultaneously arrested on Friday the thirteenth – of October, 1307. Given the preoccupation of the medieval mind with numerology, perhaps this is significant. And even if the attackers of the Templars took no account of such superstitious trifles, perhaps someone else did. For on the arguments of Baigent, Leigh and Lincoln, someone not only engineered the Templars' downfall, but gave them advance warning of it, enabling them to destroy most of their records and remove to safety their vast treasure and their sacred relics (including perhaps the shroud of Turin [see page

for the Templars' rejection of the cross and the crucifixion. Yet they fail to acknowledge the serious weakness this rejection creates in their own line of reasoning. If the Templars and their associates reject the cross and the crucifixion (for whatever reason), why should they be dedicated to preserving the secret of Jesus's physical descendants and restoring them to power? One possible explanation, advanced later by the authors themselves, is that a fake Jesus died on the cross – and that the real one escaped. Yet this does not at all seem to be the tenor of the Templars' remarks – 'Christ is a false prophet' not 'that was a false Christ'. And what in any case of the remark that the crucifix is 'too young' to be an object of veneration? There is, in fact, much other evidence to show that the Templar concerns were quite other, much older – and much more mysterious.

The Templars were also charged, both by the Catholic Church and by persistent popular rumour, that they believed the bearded heads and skulls they worshipped in secret could 'make the trees flower and the land

Right: Pope John XXIII (1881-1963), who used the same papal name as a 15th-century antipope (below). It has been argued that Pope John XXIII was sympathetic to, or even a member of, the Priory of Sion

In his mural (right) for the church of Notre Dame de France in London, Jean Cocteau (above) – allegedly Grand Master of the Priory of Sion from 1918 to 1963 – shows himself, significantly, looking *away* from the cross

39] and the mummified head of Christ) – for none of these items were ever found. Perhaps the Priory of Sion itself wanted to curb its military arm – but certainly not to have the central mystery, the treasure, or its own long-term purpose destroyed.

The number 13 plays a significant role in the mystery unfolded by Baigent, Leigh and Lincoln. From their own text, let us consider one of the many hints that cast light upon this recurrent number. Records state that the Grand Master of the Priory of Sion from 1637 to 1654 was J. Valentin Andreae. Around the beginning of the same century, the Rosicrucian movement – a mysterious fraternity claiming to possess certain 'spiritual truths' – had announced its existence in Europe, and Andrea was himself a dedicated Rosicrucian. Despite his knowledge that all heresies had for some 200 years been strictly punished by the Church, Andrea set up in Europe a network of semi-secret societies, the Christian Unions, to preserve 'knowledge' that was bound to be regarded by the orthodox church as heretical. Each of these unions was headed by an anonymous 'prince' assisted by 12 followers. This grouping is, of course, strongly reminiscent of witches' covens – the 12 men or women led by a familiar or initiate – or, of course, of the group formed by Jesus and his 12 disciples.

A particularly fascinating piece of evidence produced by Baigent, Leigh and Lincoln concerns Pope John XXIII. His choice, on his election in 1959, of the name John is a surprising one in view of the fact that a 15th-century antipope, or contestant for the papacy, had also carried the name John XXIII. After the modern Pope John's death

Pierre Plantard de Saint-Clair, who was allegedly elected Grand Master of the Priory of Sion on 17 January 1981 – and is also said to be a direct descendant of Christ

there were those who suggested that he was a member of the Rosicrucians and of the Priory of Sion. Had he adopted the name John because it was also the Christian name of Jean Cocteau, then the Grand Master of Sion? The coincidence becomes significant on consideration of a further fact: this modern Pope John decreed that Catholics now had permission to be Freemasons – a complete reversal of the Vatican's previous policy. Freemasons claim direct descent, ultimately, from the Knights Templar themselves, but also from such organisations as the Christian Unions. Moreover, Pope John proclaimed that the most important item of the whole crucifixion was not the resurrection, but the shedding of Christ's blood. This strange proclamation already turns our thoughts to the Holy Grail – the receptacle usually understood to have captured the blood Christ shed while on the cross. For Baigent, Leigh and Lincoln, however, the blood of Christ means specifically the blood*line* – the descendants – of Christ. Yet in fact, as we shall see, the implications of blood are far older and broader than these authors imagine. It will startle most Christians to learn, for instance, that the word 'sabbath' (from Akkadian *shabattu* or *shapattu*) originally means 'the festival of the menstruating Moon goddess'.

It is such seemingly unrelated themes as these that we must begin to examine. We shall discover a web of interconnecting societies, secret and public, in which one mystery is solved only to reveal another.

The king and the covens

Many primitive societies practised ritual sacrifices of their kings to ensure the continued well-being of the tribe. Could it be that this practice continued, even in Western Europe, well into historic time?

THE STORY OF THE FOUNDING of the Most Noble Order of the Garter is as follows. Edward III of England (1312-1377) was dancing – either with the Fair Maid of Kent or the Countess of Salisbury according to which tradition one follows – when his partner dropped her garter. The king immediately seized the garter and pinned it to his own leg, saying '*Honi soit qui mal y pense*' – shame to him who thinks evil of this incident. Going still further, in fulfilment of a vow to restore the Round Table of Arthur, the king then founded two groups of Garter knights, 12 for himself and 12 for the Prince of Wales, adopting as their motto *Honi soit qui mal y pense*. These two groups, plus the respective leaders, form two bands of 13. The rise of this number appears to have been deliberate: it is significant that the king's mantle as Chief of the Order is powdered over with 168 garters. These, together with the one worn on the leg, make a total of 169; that is 13 times 13.

The garter or cord as the mark of a sorcerer is known from oldest antiquity, and can be seen in prehistoric cave paintings of sorcerers. In the medieval witch trials in France, also, it was frequently stated that the leaders of each coven wore a garter as a sign of rank.

Some 40 years before the founding of the Order of the Garter, there had been among the charges levelled at the Knights Templar by the Inquisition that, when worshipping the severed heads or skulls at their secret rituals, 'they surrounded or touched each head of the aforesaid idols with small cords, which they wore around themselves next to the shirt or the flesh.'

There is even a legend linking King Arthur with the sorcerer's garter. According to local folklore, King Arthur and Guinevere sleep in a cave under the castle of Sewingshields in Northumberland. A farmer allegedly once found his way into this cave, and near the entrance saw a stone sword, a garter and a horn. He took up the sword and cut the garter, but his nerve failed when he saw the sleepers awakening. As he ran out of the cave he heard King Arthur say:

O woe befall the evil day
   that ever the witless wight was born
   who took the sword, the garter cut
   but never blew the bugle horn.

The most obvious explanation of Edward III's behaviour in the incident that led to the founding of the Order of the Garter is that he was covering up some kind of sexual liaison with the lady concerned. There is another interpretation, however: the time was marked by a number of witch trials involving members of the aristocracy in which the noble leaders went unpunished while their followers were imprisoned or executed. Edward III could have been putting under his personal protection a woman who was at risk from these infamous witch trials. He could also have been announcing publicly to a secret band of his pagan followers that he himself was the grand master of the witches they revered.

Above: the knights of the Most Noble Order of the Garter in procession to St George's chapel, Windsor. Legend says that the order was founded after King Edward III (1312–1377) picked up a garter that his dancing partner had inadvertently dropped (right). Exclaiming '*Honi soit qui mal y pense*', or 'Shame be on him who thinks evil of this incident', he picked up the garter – and went on to found the Order of the Garter, adopting his remark as its motto. The garter is an ancient sorcerers' symbol: could Edward have been announcing his sovereignty over British witches?

There is an intriguing connection between Edward III and the Knights Templar. In *The holy blood and the Holy Grail*, Michael Baigent, Richard Leigh and Henry Lincoln report a very curious incident, known as 'the cutting of the elm'. It took place in 1188, and marked the formal break between the Order of Sion and the Order of Templars, which had hitherto been synonymous. Adjacent to the Templar fortress of Gisors was a field, a place sacred since pre-Christian times, and which had often served as a meeting place for the kings of England and the kings of France. In the centre of this field was an ancient, gigantic elm. On this particular occasion a quarrel, whose details we do not know, arose between Philippe II of France and Henry II of England. A fight ensued, in which blood was shed, and one of Henry's sons, Richard Lionheart, attempted to defend the tree – but the French succeeded in cutting it down. At this point, it seems, the Order of Sion split from the Templars, changed its name to the Priory of Sion, and adopted as a sub-name 'Ormus'. *Orme* is the French for elm.

What all this signifies is impossible to say, but it seems that there is a covert connection between Henry II and the founding of the Priory of Sion. And, some 60 years later in 1252, Henry III, the grandson of Henry II, was publicly threatened by the Templars: 'So long as thou dost exercise justice, thou wilt reign. But if thou infringe it, thou wilt cease to be king.' This statement amounts to an extraordinary threat; the implication is both that the king has somehow offended the Templars, and is also somehow beholden to them. Finally, a further hundred years later, we find Henry III's great-grandson, Edward III, founding the Order of the Garter.

There are many more hints of connections between Templars, the Priory of Sion, witches and the nobility of England and France. Let us now dispense with hints and bring a whole section of the central mystery into the open.

In the 1920s Margaret Murray, a distinguished Egyptologist, enraged a previously admiring academic world with the publication of her two books *The witch cult in western Europe* and *The god of the witches*. In her view, the study of the religion of pre-Christian times had been completely neglected – this was slightly unfair to J. G. Frazer's *The golden bough* (1922) – and she proceeded to redress the balance. The standard religion of Europe and the Middle East, she claimed, had been close to what is today called witchcraft. It involved the worship of the Horned

Top: a fragment of a limestone tablet from Ur, in ancient Babylonia. The king is pouring libations to the Moon god Nannar. The religions of many ancient societies involved worship of the Moon in the form of the Horned God or Goddess – as in Celtic mythology, where Cernunnos, 'the Horned One' (above, flanked by a wolf and a stag), rules over the entire animal kingdom. The Horned God or Goddess was essentially a fertility deity, neither good nor evil. It is likely that the personification of the Satan of the Christian Church as a horned creature is the result of a deliberate attempt to stigmatise the Horned God

God or Goddess, who ruled over both good and evil, and was the creator of both. In essence the original paganism-witchcraft was a fertility religion, pre-dating the discovery of agriculture and farming methods, and concerned with producing abundance in game animals and wild plants.

In the centuries following Christ, the kings and rulers of Europe were gradually persuaded to declare their public support for Christianity, but Murray suggests that even in post-medieval times the mass of people and many of the nobility continued to worship the old gods in the old ways. Murray comments that 'even in the highest offices of the Church the priests often served the heathen deities as well as the Christian God and practised pagan rites.' Such a view is supported by the mystery labyrinths inlaid on the floors of French cathedrals, by the discovery in the 1940s of a stone penis carved inside the altar of an English church, and a complete Celtic altar bearing the names and portraits of the Celtic gods (including Cernunnos, the horned stag god, flanked by a bear) built into the choir of Notre Dame church in Paris; or even by Robert Graves's evidence, presented in *The white goddess*, that the old 13-month year was still commonly observed in medieval rural Britain.

It is against the formidable background of the wide-scale continuance of pagan tradition that we must seek to understand the Templars, the Priory of Sion, *qabalists*, Cathars, alchemists, the witches themselves and many allied manifestations.

The king of the world

Baigent, Leigh and Lincoln have demonstrated some of the many interconnections between Cathars, gnostics, Templars, *qabalists* and others. Nicolas Flamel, Grand Master of the Priory from 1398 to 1418, was also a famous alchemist. The documents found at Rennes-le-Château (see page 14) prominently feature the phrase *rex mundi* ('king of the world'). This concept is a notion central to all forms of gnosticism, of which the sect of the Cathars in France represents one variant. These sects held that God, being pure spirit and goodness, could not have produced the world, which is both material and at least partly evil. The world, Christ and mankind were held to be the product of another entity, capable of immersion in matter. This usurper god, or rex mundi, has much in common with Satan, Lucifer and ultimately with the Horned God of paganism.

Below: a ritual sacrifice of a goat, made by the Dinka tribe of the Sudan, north-east Africa, to ensure the recovery of a sick man. Most primitive tribes practise animal, and sometimes human, sacrifice. The ancient Druids of Britain were one such society; this highly romanticised engraving (below right) shows a mother's grief as her son is sacrificed during a Druid ritual

Again and again in *The holy blood and the Holy Grail*, we find references to the involvement of Jewish thinkers in all these mystery and semi-mystery movements, including persons such as Nostradamus himself. And not only outright mystical traditions like the Jewish *qabalah* are involved. Orthodox Judaism also has many connections with the matters we have been discussing. For example, orthodox Jewish thought holds there to be 13 central qualities to God. These (derived from Exodus 34:6-7) are: (1) Lord, (2) God, (3) merciful, (4) gracious, (5) long-suffering, (6) abundant in goodness, (7) abundant in truth, (8) keeping mercy, (9) keeping faith to the thousandth generation, (10) forgiving iniquity, (11) forgiving transgressions, (12) forgiving sin, and (13) acquitting. This list obviously involves some forcing to arrive at the number 13. These 13 attributes form the central part of all Jewish penitential prayers.

The frequency and power of the number seven in both Judaism and Christianity are manifest; the sacred Jewish seven-branched candlestick, the *menorah*, which is described as 'the seven eyes of God which range through the whole earth' and 'the seven stars', appears to have some connection with the seven stars of the Plough – part of the Great Bear constellation.

Unlike the number seven, however, the number 13 seems to have undergone considerable purging from the text of the Bible.

Left: detail of a carving showing the murder of Thomas à Becket in 1170. The anthropologist Margaret Murray has suggested that the ancient practice of ritually sacrificing important figures in order to ensure continued fertility of crops and livestock continued into historic times – and that among its victims were Becket and (right) William Rufus (1087–1100), who died in suspicious circumstances while hunting. There is a further intriguing possibility: that the ritual murderers are guardians of the old religion, descendants of the last king of the Merovingian dynasty, Dagobert II – whose trepanned skull (below right) is now lodged in a convent at Mons, Belgium – himself a descendant of Christ

Much to the point here is also that the words 'blood', 'bless' and 'blossom' all come from the same root: again the fertility element is quite clear.

Could this be a key to the puzzle? Perhaps. The many strands of the central mystery at last begin to form a coherent and recognisable pattern.

New ships were originally sanctified by sacrifice; and we still bless a new ship by breaking a bottle of champagne over the bows. The victim was doubtless once a human being – for human sacrifice was undoubtedly at the heart of the old religion. The most important sacrifice of all was that of the king. The chosen king had to die – originally every year, subsequently every seventh or ninth year – in order to ensure the continuing fertility of the tribe itself, of the game and the wild plants. Probably Murray's most outrageous claim is that many kings and notables of historical times were ritually killed by the witch cult. She cites, in Britain, King Edmund (AD 946), Edmund Ironside (1016), William Rufus (1100) and Thomas à Becket (1170); and in France Joan of Arc (1431) and Gilles de Rais (1440). Could it be that such ritual killings did indeed continue in the heart of Western society far into historic time?

Nevertheless, it is clear, for instance, that Israel is regarded as yet another group of 13 – Jacob and his 12 sons. As one religion succeeds another, those elements of the old religion that can be assimilated become part of the new religion; the remaining elements are strongly suppressed. It seems reasonable to suppose that the purging of the number 13 from the Bible indicates that it was of significance in the religion that Judaism, and later Christianity, replaced – perhaps the old pagan religion of Moon worship, in which the number 13, the number of full or new moons in the 13-month year, was held in great reverence.

Blood sacrifice

Another piece of evidence for the nature of the old religion, not cited by Baigent, Leigh and Lincoln, is the persistent medieval story that Jews used the blood of a Christian child to make their Passover bread. Of course, they did nothing of the kind. The fact of the matter is that Jews are forbidden to consume blood in any form, so that all meat must be bled dry by ritual slaughter, and an egg with a speck of blood in it must be thrown away. But this very strong prohibition of blood in the Jewish religion suggests that back in pagan times blood was at the very centre of their religious practice. Margaret Murray, indeed, assures us of the importance of allowing the blood of a human sacrifice to strike the earth in pagan ritual.

Murder by moonlight

Close examination of the Bible yields evidence of an attempt to suppress an ancient tradition of Moon worship. This chapter presents the remarkable hypothesis that dim but potent echoes of this religion still persist

WHAT WAS THE NATURE of the old religion that was supplanted by Judaism? We have seen that it was probably a fertility religion in which worship of the Moon played an important part (see page 90). This is strongly implied by certain evidence from the Bible. A new religion generally suppresses those elements of the religion it supplants that it cannot absorb, and the fact that the number 13 appears to have undergone a considerable purging from the Old Testament suggests that 13 may have had some significance in the old religion. Thirteen is the number of houses in the Moon zodiac – it is the number of full or new Moons in the solar year – and is therefore of central importance in Moon worship.

There are passages in the Old Testament that make it clear that a flourishing tradition of Moon worship existed alongside Judaism. In Isaiah 1:13-14, for example, God, speaking through the prophet, says:

> Bring no more vain oblations; incense is an abomination to me; the new moons and sabbaths, the calling of assemblies, I cannot away with; it is iniquity, even the solemn meeting.
> Your new moons and your appointed feasts my soul hateth: they are a trouble unto me; I am weary to bear them.

And in Hosea 2:11, speaking of the iniquitous state of Judaism, he says:

> I will also cause all her mirth to cease, her feast days, her new moons, and her sabbaths, and all her solemn feasts.

Turning to what at first seems to be entirely different evidence, there are some important connections between the numbers 7 – which retains an important place in the Bible – and 13, which has been largely purged. Seven is the midpoint between 1 and 13:

$$1\ 2\ 3\ 4\ 5\ 6\ 7\ 8\ 9\ 10\ 11\ 12\ 13$$

Midpoints are extremely important in all occult thought – midnight, the midwinter solstice, midsummer's day, for instance. The main origins of this general concern about midpoints are probably midwinter (will the slain Sun live again this year?) and midnight (will the hidden Sun come back to us once more?).

The midpoint between one and seven is four, thus:

$$1\ 2\ 3\ 4\ 5\ 6\ 7$$

Multiplying the two mid-numbers and 13 itself together, $7 \times 4 \times 13$, gives 364 – the number of days in a full year – or almost. The number we need is 365 – and this is why, Robert Graves tells us, ancient legends refer not to a year, but to a year and a day $(364 + 1)$. There is more: the number of quarters of the Moon, $4 \times 7 = 28$; and 28, is of course, the average length of the female menstrual cycle.

Ancient Egyptian tombs, dating back to around 3000 BC, contain some very curious magical implements or 'chess boards'. On these boards there is room only for the pieces themselves – none for moving them. There are always either 7 or 13 pieces along each side of the board – 49 or 169 pieces altogether – and, more significant, the pieces themselves are always in the shape of half-moons. Osiris, to whose cult these items belong, was one instance of a 'Horned God', and his sister Isis was a 'Horned Goddess' (see page 89). But Robert Graves tells us that Isis was not originally the sister of Osiris but his mother, and that she ruled before him.

The American researcher James Vogh, aware that there might be a Moon zodiac of greater antiquity than the familiar Sun zodiac, set out to discover the thirteenth sign of the Moon zodiac. He found it to be Arachne, the Cretan spider goddess. One of

his major pieces of evidence was a mosaic zodiac from a Jewish gnostic synagogue, Beth Alpha, in the Jezreel Valley in Israel. It is clear that this has been altered from a 13-house to a 12-house zodiac. In the middle sits a spider-like figure, Arachne, with 13 items in her headdress and the crescent Moon on her left shoulder.

Vogh also became fascinated by the many ancient legends in which threads are used to lead people out of labyrinths, and their connections with spiders' webs – and, via them, with the spider goddess Arachne. One of the most important labyrinths of the ancient world was that of Knossos, which flourished with the Minoan civilisation around 2500 BC. At the centre of the labyrinth was said to live the strange creature known as the Minotaur, the offspring of a bull and of the wife of Minos, the king of

Top: a spider's web, symbol of delusion and captivity. Researcher James Vogh believes he has discovered the thirteenth sign of the Moon zodiac – that of the spider goddess Arachne, shown at the centre of a zodiac from the gnostic synagogue at Beth Alpha (above)

Left: the Immaculate Conception, by Murillo (1617–1682). The Virgin Mary is traditionally shown trampling a crescent Moon. Could this be an indication that Christianity superseded a religion of Moon worship?

Crete, herself the daughter of the Moon. Vogh took the name *Minotaur*, split it and reversed the order of the pieces. He now had *taur* and *min* – with the *o*, he conjectured, perhaps representing the Moon. From this and other evidence, advanced in his book *Arachne rising: the thirteenth sign* (1977), he deduces that the sign of Arachne must originally have fallen between the two consecutive signs of Taurus and Gemini.

Many lines of evidence suggest that the spider goddess, the Moon goddess, and the universal earth mother – who seems to have made her appearance somewhat later than these two – are one and the same. But perhaps of more immediate importance is Vogh's suggestion that the many instances of pre-Christian crosses are actually stylised spiders. The variant of the cross we call the swastika is perhaps the most literally suggestive of the spider; and Vogh has many spider amulets from North America with a cross in a circle drawn upon their backs.

Baleful Moon dew

As previously mentioned, Moon and menstruation are derived from the same root, and scientific study has shown that the Moon is closely related to the female menstrual cycle. A menstruating woman is a fertile woman, and few things were more important to ancient peoples than a regular supply of new babies to ensure the continued existence of the tribe. Women also apparently dream more at menstruation than at other times, but in any case the connections between menstruation and mysticism are legion. Robert Graves tells us that 'the baleful moon dew of the witches of Thessaly was a girl's first menstrual blood taken during an eclipse of the moon.' The sabbath, both the Christian and the witches' version, was originally the festival of the Moon goddess's menstruation. All early peoples – Europeans, Asians, North and South American Indians, Africans and Australian Aborigines – believed that the red soil found throughout the world was the blood of the Moon goddess shed when giving birth to the planet Earth. This red soil is everywhere regarded as a magical substance. Some authors have seen among its various descendants the ash of Ash Wednesday, and the 'red powder' that, in many folk tales from all over Europe, could turn base metals into gold or silver.

It seems much more likely, however, that this belief is a confused memory of the sacrificial blood and the menstrual blood of women, and the goddess who turned the dead land of winter into the gold of summer and autumn. The so-called noble metals of the alchemists, gold and silver, do happen also to be the colours of the Sun and Moon.

In summary, it seems we have evidence of a garbled and distorted memory of a religion

Above: a carving of the ancient fertility goddess, known as a Sheila-na-gig, being seduced by the Lord of the Underworld, on the porch of the church of St Mary, Whittlesford, Cambridgeshire. Fertility is immensely important in all primitive societies – the face of this Brazilian girl (left) has been smeared with red ochre to ensure her fertility; it is a symbol of the blood that, her tribe believes, was shed by the Earth mother when she was giving birth to the Earth. In his book *The white goddess*, Robert Graves (below) argues that the idea of a fertility goddess pre-dates notions of male gods – and the Moon is perhaps the oldest fertility goddess

knights are loyal except the rebellious and traitorous Mordred. While Arthur is absent, Mordred usurps the kingdom and marries Guinevere, Arthur's wife. On Arthur's return, he and Mordred fight, and deal each other mortal wounds. Arthur is said not to be dead, however, but only sleeping. One day he will awake and return to lead his people once more.

In Scandinavian mythology, the story of the death of Baldur, the most loved of the gods, is as follows. A banquet is held in Valhalla to which 12 of the gods have been invited. While the feast is in progress Loki, the spirit of strife and mischief, who has not been invited, nevertheless turns up as the thirteenth guest. He gives blind Hoder an arrow of mistletoe, and gets him to shoot it. It kills Baldur. In the Saxon version of the story, Baldur is resurrected, and the golden age of mankind begins.

The story of Christ's crucifixion is this. Christ leads a band of 12 disciples – making a band of 13 altogether. Christ is betrayed by a

of enormous antiquity – a fertility religion in which worship of the Moon played a central part.

Let us now turn our attention to a number of legends and fairy tales.

The story of Sleeping Beauty is as follows. A great king invites 12 good fairies to attend the christening of his daughter. Each bestows a blessing on the child. But a thirteenth, evil, fairy, who has not been invited, now appears and curses the child with death if she should ever prick her finger. Despite all precautions, she does, and falls into a permanent sleep. All around her, the castle and its lands also fall dead. One day, however, a brave knight finds his way to the castle, and at his kiss the princess and her lands come once again to life.

King Arthur of Britain has in his castle a round table at which he sits with his 12 most favoured knights – a total of 13. All the

King Arthur and Mordred fight their battle to the death (above left); Loki incites the blind Hoder to kill Baldur (above right); the Sleeping Beauty is awakened by a kiss (left); and Christ is betrayed by Judas (below left). In all these stories, the 'best' or most beloved member of a group is killed by the weakest – but comes to life again, heralding a period of joy and well-being. These stories may all mirror the drama of the natural year, in which, in the short or 'weak' lunar month – at the winter solstice – the Sun is 'betrayed' and 'dies', only to come to life again, bringing summer and plenty

Below: the seal of the English Templars, bearing the device of the crescent Moon – the beginning, and perhaps the end, of the mysteries unravelled in the 1982 bestseller *The holy blood and the Holy Grail*

weak and treacherous member of the group, Judas, and is executed. Nevertheless, two days later he has risen from the dead. Christ's death and resurrection signal redemption for mankind and the promise of eternal life.

The parallels in these stories are obvious. In each of them, the most beloved is killed by the one evil or weak member of a group of 13. The most beloved dies and desolation follows. But the most beloved comes to life again, and all will be well once more.

It seems clear that these stories are all metaphorical representations of the cycle of the year. They are all the story of the Sun who is killed each year by the Moon, but is then immediately resurrected by her to bring another golden summer. The Moon year contains only twelve and a half complete cycles of the Moon. The thirteenth lunar month is therefore short and 'weak'. It is in this 'weak' month that the Sun dies.

Confirmation of this interpretation comes from the Saxon version of the Baldur story, where Baldur and Hoder die fighting for the hand of the virgin Moon. Moreover, in Scandinavian mythology Baldur is the 'god of the summer sunlight', whereas Hoder represents 'darkness and winter'.

The authors of *The holy blood and the Holy Grail* are quite emphatic that Mary Magdalene's role in the Bible story has been heavily censored (see page 85) – and I entirely agree with them. I go further however: I believe she is the representative of a cult of Moon worship, and that the story of Christ's crucifixion is the story of a ritual killing, a confused relic of a time when sacrifice of the king was believed necessary to ensure the continued fertility of the land and tribe. The Priory of Sion, for whose existence Michael Baigent, Richard Leigh and Henry Lincoln argue so persuasively, is the guardian of this ancient tradition of Moon worship – very old, very powerful and still flourishing to this day right at the centre of Western civilisation.

Index